THE POWER TO FORGIVE

ESCAPING
Tragedy

THE POWER TO FORGIVE

ESCAPING
Tragedy

MAXINE EVANS GRAY

ARPress
ILLUMINATING IDEAS
EMPOWERING VOICES

ARPress
45 Dan Road Suite 5
Canton MA 02021

Hotline: 1(888) 821-0229
Fax: 1(508) 545-7580

Ordering Information:
Quantity sales. Special discounts are available on quantity purchases by corporations, associations, and others. For details, contact the publisher at the address above.

Printed in the United States of America.

ISBN-13:   Paperback   979-8-89389-877-4
             eBook   979-8-89389-878-1

Library of Congress Control Number: 2024923822

Table of Contents

Escaping Tragedy

Introduction

To whom you forgive anything, I forgive also: for if I forgave anything, to whom I forgave it, for your sakes forgave I it in the person of Christ, Lest Satan should get an advantage of us: for we are not ignorant of his devices.

2 Corinthians 2:10-11.

I was strong during the days after her death and even during her Homegoing Service. My surviving sisters and I had learned to smile in public and cry privately. At the service I stood on the church platform, spoke fondly of our sister boldly, and shared great episodes of our crazy adventures. They all laughed amidst the tears. We were able to continue the service calmly. Yet as I saw the body of my baby sister being lowered into the ground in the coffin that signified to my inner being that she would never return, my strength dissipated, and the tears broke through! I cried bitterly and went into instant grief and great pain that lasted for months. In spite of the grief, I felt the overwhelming desire to see to it that the invisible creature that was assigned to destroy my family and me would himself be destroyed. I am on a mission.

I had heard about generational curses, but it had never dawned on me that I was caught in the middle of a spiritual and vicious dog fight until I saw the gruesome pattern of tragedies that seemed to occur in cycles. Though varied accounts of the reasons for these tragedies were being handed down from generation to generation, I could not understand why so many of my closest relatives and friends were being tormented and killed by unseen forces in rural Copiah County, Mississippi.

After seeing coffin after coffin lowered into the ground and family members almost out of their minds with grief, I knew I had to have answers! My family! My knowledge of it began with the untimely death of my paternal grandfather, whom I never had the privilege of knowing; and afterwards this unseen villain claimed uncles, brothers, sisters, cousins, and even my mother! I sought for answers and begged the God, whom I also could not see, to tell me how to escape and to help others escape from such a vicious cycle of death and destruction! I cried out, "God, what has my family done that is so horrible?! How can this be stopped?!"

Later in my life as a born again believer in Christ, the Lord began to speak to me about the power of the Fourth Generation—that spell-breaking generation. I had repented of my sins, but I didn't experience the change I so desperately needed until I learned about the authority that lies within that powerful force called FORGIVENESS.

This is for my family and for the world.

Papa's Song

(Matt and Celie Powell)

In October of 2014 my youngest sister Patricia, whom we affectionately call Ann, very persuasively and persistently talked me into adjusting my unusually heavy schedule to take a road trip with her to the wooded place where my mother grew up. She was infatuated with seeing everything again, but would not have dared to go by herself. Her persistence paid off. I tabled everything and chauffeured her to rural Copiah County, Mississippi. As we passed by some of the old houses that had stood the test of time, memories began to pour into our hearts. It was the best road trip I could have ever invested in! It was the last one that I would take with her.

The old house was at the end of a very narrow path with thick woods on both sides. We were both quite frightened, but dared to keep driving deeper and deeper into the wooded area until finally we saw the old house. As I glared at the growth of weeds and trees in the place that was once clean and clear, I was taken back into time and could hear and see Mama and her sisters and brothers running, laughing, and singing around that old wood cabin.

I also saw their tired bodies inside the house after a long day of work in the fields, bathed, well-fed, and more than ready to lie down on the soft hand-made mattresses filled with cotton straight from the fields. After everyone was clean and refreshed, the lamps were blown out, and deep darkness filled the house.

A lamp was only relit when one of them had to go to the outhouse. Snakes and other critters were known to creep around the farm. Neither of them was afraid. They were all taught how to protect themselves from those lurking nighttime predators.

I could also hear the tears and sense the tragic stories that they took to the grave with them. They were very private and believed in protecting the reputation of one another. They were not gossipers at all and stood together through thick and thin.

I heard the lullabies of raindrops as they harmoniously in crescendo style lovingly teased the tin roof of the old wood house, and the rumbling of soft thunder that filled the house with unbelievable peace and quiet. "Sleep…sleep…sleep", whispered the rain to a large family consisting of a tired, aging man, his dedicated wife, and their eleven children. No lights were on, except one kerosene lamp that my grandfather used to read his worn out Bible and to sing from his hymnal in spite of how tired he was. It was a ritual for him to have daily devotions.

This was my mother's home for 16 years. Her father and mother had successfully endured the Great Depression and found a bit of wealth and prosperity. The farm was large, and they had much land for the horses, cattle, chickens, turkeys, and hunting hound dogs that had the loudest yelp you ever want to hear! Now there's only silence.

Located in the deep woods of Copiah County, the house my grandfather built for his large family remarkably holds such rich history and overcoming love! The swing that we loved dearly was fastened securely to the strong beam of the roof on the right side of the house and could hold two people. Swinging in that old swing was one of the highlights of my visits. Otherwise, I really was afraid of visiting Big Mama and Papa, because of the animals and critters.

Mama's wise father chose a spot on his land where there was water and plenty of persimmon trees, plum trees, and even fig trees. He cautioned us about choosing the right persimmons to eat from the tree that stood very stately in front of the house adjacent to the well. We found out the hard way that the wrong persimmons would immediately dry up the saliva in our mouths and cause our lips to pucker!

The well he dug was located right in front of the house. He and others in that day knew how to use a "diviner's rod" to locate water. I had seen my dad and uncle do it several times, but when I tried it, nothing ever happened! Yet I saw the rod quiver as they pointed it toward the earth. There they would dig and dig, until finally water began to gush! To me that was nothing short of miraculous!

There was the potato house where they stored sweet potatoes and canned goods that was located underneath the back of the main structure of the house. I've dreamed many times about this being some kind of secret underground series of chambers that housed great riches! A hen house in the back held many chickens that kept the family with fresh eggs. I was afraid to go back there! They also were ornery!

Her father, Madison Powell, was nicknamed Matt, but we all called him "Papa." The love of his life was Big Mama, Celia Cammack-Powell. He was much older than his orphaned child bride, whom he married when she was the tender age of 14. She was being reared by an older sister who was very strict. Marrying Papa was her escape and delight. I felt that may have been the reason she seemed to have been more withdrawn than Papa. Nevertheless, she was nice to us and had this beautiful, quiet smile! All that I was graced to hear about this loving couple was that they were totally dedicated to each other.

Big Mama was relatively meek and soft spoken, yet authoritative. I noticed that she and the family never talked around us or anyone at all about problems they may have encountered. Because of her silence and solemn personality, I was afraid of her, but not of Papa who was more open, laughable, and talkative. Mama would so often tell of what a good person she was and how much she loved her. Oh, but we couldn't touch her extremely neat and clean bed covered with beautiful quilts that she skillfully hand-made. If we even put a finger on it, we would get swatted hard by her long platted switch. I most gladly complied to her!

Papa made sure that his children were as properly schooled as possible in those early days of the birthing of rights and liberties for "negroes" in that area in Mississippi that was very far behind most of the nation! They all went to one school called Ebenezer, a one-room structure that housed children of all ages. Mama had many stories to tell us about the children at Ebenezer who were just basically unintellectual, because most

5

of their time was spent in the fields and in the woods logging. So they enjoyed hearing one another stammer. Mama and her brothers and sisters were keen and very intelligent in spite of the long days in the fields. They inherited it from their parents.

Mama and all her siblings were also natural story tellers! These talented and hilarious individuals could have easily become best-selling authors or even singing prodigies; yet they kept their gifts to themselves and just sang very harmonious acapella and told crazy, yet true, stories to one another and the few visiting friends they had, demonstrating and making mocking sounds as they laughingly told their side-splitting stories even at times when they toiled in the fields as the summer sun angrily scorched their skin.

I loved the double fire place that warmed that room and the adjourning room that the girls slept in. I can still catch a whiff of the aromatic fragrance of burning pieces of fresh pine that were used for kindling. The third room was the boys' room. They had no fireplace in their room, but the heat from the other rooms and the kitchen was sufficient.

There was no electricity in that wooden cabin. Kerosene lamps lit up the house, and a wood stove that gave the food a funny after-taste (which I wasn't very fond of) sat in the corner of the kitchen in the four-room cabin. Big Mama expertly produced cakes, biscuits, and all kinds of goodies from that funny looking black contraption! That I loved! My small frame provoked Big Mama to make sure that I ate, but did not force me to eat the squirrel, rabbit, or possum meats that she knew I despised the thought of! Chicken was my favorite; so they made sure that they had fried chicken on hand for me to eat during my visits with my parents. I could hear the loud cackles of the chickens as Papa chose which one of them would die for the family's dinner! I was terrified!

They were all church-goers; they didn't have a choice! The family church was Salem Missionary Baptist Church, also located in the deep woods; and they also attended **Taylor Grove Union at Home**, established by Papa, where Christian neighbors, friends, and loved ones came together and paid dues so that if any of them died or became ill, the Union would be able to help with burial and other expenses. Their dues were 25 cents annually. How I long for those days!

It was always so hot at Taylor's Grove! Everyone knew to grab a paper fan when entering. It didn't help much though! The meetings never lasted very long, thank God! Papa always had the lengthiest speech, and I never really understood what he was saying until at the end he would say, "And I thank you!" I then knew I could finally go home. The Union is still in operation now, and the dues have not much changed! They are no longer having meetings in that one-room, sweltering building, but Papa's Union lives!

People said that Papa was a mean man in his earlier life. I never witnessed this side of Papa, because before I was born, our Papa found Jesus. All that I saw was this gentle, loving, slightly bent over old man who walked with a cane, who loved to preach to us in private, but never in public. Some who knew him called him a "jack legged preacher." He never confessed the ministry; yet he was indeed a minister! I often wonder what it was that prevented him from taking to the pulpit. If these stories of his being a bad man are true, it could account for his reluctance to confess a calling that was definitely present in his life. Then again maybe it was just for our family and me.

When we would go for a visit, we were compelled to sit for what seemed to be an eternity and listen to him read and expound on scripture. Then we would very carefully look through the old hymn book he and Big Mama kept safely in the house, and we would sing. Our favorite song was "His Eye is on the Sparrow." That seemed to have been one of his favorite as well! We purposefully choose that song and would only make it as far as one line in it before he would grab the book and say, "Let me show you how to sing it, Babe; His eye-- is on-- the sparruuuu! And I know he's watching meeee!" We very quietly and carefully laughed among one another and waited until we were in safe distance from the house toward our own home before we really let go and laughed! Mama and Daddy joined in the laughter.

We would not have dared laugh in his face, because Mama had told us of the trouble her older sister Aunt Thelma fell into when she had to hold the lamp as he sang. Everyone else was at safe laughing distance, and she knew they were having fun at her expense. All of a sudden she could hold her bubbling laughter no longer, and her exploding breath blew out the lamp! She got it good! Therefore we grandchildren were very careful to not annoy him in any kind of way with our laughter.

Yet we were never treated unkindly by him. He was a humorous man in his own special way. He would tell a "funny", then give out a laugh that made the joke he told funnier! Sounding like he was about to cough, he would loudly emit, "Hchah!!!" Then the laughter from him was over! Sometimes he would make us laugh, and then say, "I ain't jokin witcha, Babe!" Then we became silent. We knew then that he was going into preacher's mode. He could talk about God for hours…and hours… and hours, or so it seemed that long to us!

He was authoritative and shrewd in business and prospered without revealing it to the world. Acres and acres of land belonged to him, and he used his children and a few hired hands to till the land and work the fields from sunup to sundown. He did not waste time with lazy people. Only those who were willing to work hard were hired by him.

Whenever we would visit, those hound dogs would tell on us! They were Papa's own alarm system in the back woods, and his company when he went hunting. Yowls could be heard about a mile away as they alerted Papa and Big Mama that company was coming. As we drove down the dusty road to the wooden, unpainted cabin, fear would grip my heart as all the animals and fowls scurried toward the car in attack mode, or so I thought! I definitely remember the crabby roosters, hens, "ginnies" or dwarf chickens, cantankerous turkeys, and loud, ill-tempered bloodhounds! The turkeys would gobble loudly as they ran toward us! It seemed as though everything on the farm sent welcome greetings that I interpreted as no-trespassing signals! The cattle and horses seemed to have evil attitudes! I now feel that it was not at all the animals, but rather the great fear my younger sister, brother, and I had for them! My overactive imagination could only see them as harmful, dangerous creatures!

My sister's and my loud screams as we jumped back into the car caused Papa to run with a limp and grab us before we encountered any of them. He would laughingly say, "They won't do nothing to you, Babe!" We were never convinced of that! We held on to his waist until we made it to the tall porch of the house. Our older sisters and brothers didn't go with us to visit, so we had to rely on Mama and Daddy who were not afraid at all and actually walked away from the car laughing at us. It was never funny to us!

He loved his grandchildren and always smiled at the boys and greeted them, "Hey there, Papa-Stoppa!!!" We would all laugh as we were led into the quaint cabin he shared with our grandmother. Because of his strength of character, shrewd business capabilities, and deep Christian virtue, I knew that his story is the answer to the questions I have about the curses.

Sometimes Mama and Daddy would go to work in the fields for Papa, and she would leave her three youngest children—my little sister Ann who was five years my younger, my baby brother Melvin who was three years younger than I, and me, with Big Mama. That's when my younger siblings and I learned more about her; when we cried for Mama, in my imagination she would become Attila the Hun!

She was very heavy handed and insisted on combing my hair! I was extremely tender-headed and had moderately long, very thick and coarse black hair! My sister had sandy red hair, almost as red as my father's. Yet Big Mama was always attracted to the cold black untamed hair on my head! They didn't use hair brushes then, but she rather combed the tangles out mercilessly! She sternly but quietly told me to be quiet; I certainly obeyed with slight sniffles. She kept switches close by, and they were so long that no one could get away! I never tested it! I stayed quiet and submissive! She never whipped me. I believe that she held back on me because of my injuries. Hooray for the injuries! My scalp would be sore for days.

She wasn't so hard on my baby sister. She seemed to sense that Ann needed that special love and affection, especially being the youngest of seven children and born at a traumatic time in Mama's life. She would take her into her arms, sit in the old wooden rocking chair that sat close to the fireplace, and rock her to sleep while singing a sweet hymn. She had a beautiful soft soprano voice that she passed down to my Mama, whose voice was an octave lower, yet very calming and peaceful. I sat quietly on the floor and listened to Big Mama's melodies until I too became very sleepy. My brother Melvin tried to test her with movement, but he too fell under her seeming spell and went to sleep.

She loved her husband and children very much though; and Uncle Thomas, whom they called Brother, loved to make her laugh. He teased her a lot, and she would laughingly swat at him with her long platted switch. One day she swung at him and accidentally hit her first granddaughter, putting her eye out. Big Mama never forgave herself; and when Mama told us about the accident and the overwhelming grief it brought to Big Mama, we then understood her pain and loved her even the more. I never saw her as the mean grandmother again. I always tried to do something special for her to make her smile. She did smile. I knew that she loved me.

vwPapa was generous, soft and tender toward us, yet he meant what he said. His keen intellect and business marketing skills gained him much favor in Copiah County and surrounding areas. He really was who we would now call a big wheel, but his demeanor did not show it. He was just a man who loved his God and his family. He was good-looking, good-hearted and humorous.

Phyllis Powell

I know that Papa loved his wife, children, and especially his grandchildren very much, but believed in strict discipline. Papa and his siblings had endured intense childhood discipline from their father and mother in slavery and post-slavery days, which would have become a generational curse; but Papa stole away to Jesus and the freedom of forgiveness, thus ending the curse that sought for his family. I heard a little about his father's wrath and knew that God had performed a great miracle on my loving grandfather!

I never had the chance to meet Papa's mother and father, William and Phyllis Powell. It was seemingly customary during that time for parents to actually beat their children into obedience. I really feel strongly that it stemmed from the cruelty of slavery that lingered even after the Civil War and the Emancipation. Anger still ruled many of their hearts. Some indeed escaped the prisons of plantation living, but only a few escaped the prisons of hostility and unforgiveness! Just like Papa, there were indeed some who learned to steal away from their inner pains and the memories of cruelty through songs of worship and praise to God.

Papa stayed busy both inside and outside of the house. Then he would walk with his home-made cane that he used to support his legs that ached from arthritis to the back porch and look up into the sky. The sun told him the time. I often wondered how the sun spoke to them! He would reach up for a bull horn that hung from the outside wall in back of the house and would blow one long blast, then short ones repeatedly. All of a sudden many dusty workers, including my mama, would appear seemingly out of nowhere and wash their hands. It was lunch time! The sun was in the middle of the sky! Noon! I was so glad to see Mama, because I was scared of the animals and Big Mama!

Papa's mode of transportation was a horse-drawn wagon. He chose to live the way he had since a child, and nobody could convince him to upgrade. When everybody drove to church in their cars, Papa would be seen suited up and walking with his cane or riding in his horse-driven wagon. I used to love to ride on the wagon, and on the horse-driven slide that was used in the fields to cart vegetables. As long as I was behind the horse and not vice versa, I felt relatively safe.

My mama's family worked long, hard hours in the fields and many times used lamps to finish their jobs. Then they canned their harvests and stored them, and packed plenty of potatoes, placing them in a structure that they called the potato house, which was actually somewhat like a basement underneath the main structure of the house. Big Mama taught Mama to make homemade jelly, molasses, and other great treats. Winters were long then, but spent securely because of goodness of the summer. They always had plenty to eat, but they had to work hard for it!

They all out-grew the farm and soon went in many different directions. Yet when the name Powell is mentioned, people automatically stand at attention! Respect, admiration, and love flow in the many hearts that have been touched by Matt Powell and his family. There was indeed something so very special about Papa and Big Mama! As I grew older, married, and bore many children of my own, I yearned to know more about the peaceful Jesus that Papa knew.

Big Mama died of colon cancer in 1968; she was in her 70's. That was one of the strange events that I will speak of later in my writings. Papa lived on until he was 96. We were hoping that he would have seen his

100th birthday, but he was ready to go home to reunite with Big Mama. I was to see more of Papa in my dreams and visions, and would ponder them in my heart. They were all about secret wealth. I feel him strongly as I write this very brief account of his life.

That old house still stands after so many years, and so do the memories of my grandfather and grandmother and the peace they shared with the community. I am extremely proud to be their grandchild!

Celie's Song

Mama eloped with Carvin Evans after high school. He didn't like his name at all and renamed himself Crosby. My mother also changed her first name. She was swept off her feet by the short, stumpy, red faced, red haired, but handsome, farmer who stole her away in the night with the aid of friends. They knew that, if caught, her Papa would have buck-shot him for sure! They escaped safely, and Celie Powell secretly became Mrs. Celia Marie Evans in 1942.

The loss of her first two babies often saddened her, but she would always come out fighting! Yet she always noted to us that she was the mother of nine children instead of seven. I was her seventh. She somewhat overcame the miscarriage, but it was very hard for her to move on after such a difficult delivery of little Sarah who was already deceased. She cried a lot after she was finally told that her little girl was gone. She continued to grieve for both babies she lost even after having seven more who did survive. I was number seven out of nine pregnancies.

Daddy had a house built for Mama on farm land in Copiah County, Mississippi, near Crystal Springs, Mississippi, where I was born and raised. The house was about a fourth of a mile from my widowed grandmother's house. She had given him the land to build, which became a curse to my mother because of the nearness to my dad's family.

The farm was small, but adequate. Daddy had a fair amount of land and was to inherit even more. I fondly remember that big house that was quite different from the house where Mama grew up. There was a large living room, dining room, and a kitchen on the left side of the house. In back of the kitchen was a smoke house attached that was actually part of the back porch. I would peep through a crack in the door, too afraid to enter, and see all kinds of meat hanging from the ceiling of the smoke house.

On the other side of the house was first the master bedroom with windows that gave an overview of the hedge trees, the china berry trees, and the large brick pillars that sat on each side of the long porch. Then there was the bathroom with no plumbing for years. Daddy had to wait until he could afford a bathtub and a commode. So we had to use that stinking outhouse or go into the woods to conduct our "business." We did not have running water, and our bathroom was that old outhouse that I hated! Snakes, lizards, frogs and all kinds of creepy critters frequented it!

Some of the best times I had while at home with Mama and Daddy were the sessions she hosted when we all would gather around the old wooden heater that was situated almost in the center of the large master bedroom. We would gobble down Mama's famous teacakes while she quilted and told us some of her hand-me-down stories that I am sharing now. Mama used this gift of storytelling often after she married Daddy to invoke pleasant laughter upon her seven living babies when we were sad about anything, especially the hard farm work. Mama would not allow anyone around her to be depressed. She always fought off her own grief with her gift of storytelling.

I was one of her greatest challenges. The puniest of all her children, I could not do the work that the others could. I have uncanny recollections of my days of infancy when I cried a whole lot! Mama would crush aspirin, put it in a spoon, add milk to it, and feed it to me. I cried more! Then the aspirin affected me, and I went into calm repose.

I also did not walk for a very long time. My grandmother thought that I was impotent and told Mama to bathe me in dirty dishwater to heal my legs. Mama questioned it but did what she said to no avail. One day when I was almost two years old, I just rose up from the floor and walked perfectly. They all screamed with excitement! I was not impotent after all; I was just afraid to walk!

Prayer was one of Mama's favorite weapons! At times I would see my daddy, who was not very religious, but definitely a believer in God, follow her pattern and bow and pray for a few seconds. I did the same, not knowing whether He heard me or not; I only knew that He indeed is God, and I longed to be close to him as was my mama. I only prayed for forgiveness for my many sins, but never interceding for my family. I felt that I could not do that. Though I was called the good girl of the family, I inwardly felt that I was too much the sinner to pray effectively for anyone, including myself.

Mama could work from sun up to sundown and never show weariness. She endured much grief, shame, oppression, and betrayal; yet she remained strong, loving, and full of integrity. I yearned to know her secret. Now I know why she could continue to work even with overbearing pain in her heart! She would sing and pray to God! You could hear her beautiful high-alto voice singing even in the distance on that country road that I and six other siblings desperately desired to leave. One of her favorite songs touched many hearts.

Use me, Lord, in thy service. Draw me nearer every day.
I am willing, Lord, to run all the way!
If I stumble while I'm trying, don't be angry; let me stay.
Because I'm willing, Lord, to run all the way!
Pained by heartaches, scorned by loved ones; A little sunshine I recall.
There are mountains in my life so hard to climb!
But I promise I'll keep climbing if you'll only let me stay
Because I'm willing, Lord, to run all the way!

Mama also had a lifelong best friend, our neighbor Ms. Agnes Taylor, my best friend's mother. Their friendship was a seed sown into her life by the God she prayed to daily. It was Ms. Agnes who kept her laughing and looking forward to the next laughter they would share. She had other children who were also best friends with my siblings and me.

Her stories were also powerful tools. She hated to see anyone browbeaten or suffering, so she would come up with a funny story that would have everyone in stitches. We learned from her to laugh even when situations become dire. My baby brother suffered with epileptic seizures, and I was crippled. My daddy was gone a lot. Much distress was in the house, but Mama had learned from Papa and Big Mama how to deal with the pressure. Then when she could take no more, she would compel my daddy to drive her to see her mama—her greatest consolation. Big Mama knew even when my tiny understanding didn't. They would never talk around us, so I never knew all that was going on until my mom's twilight.

She began to open up and share details with me when she saw that God was in control of my life.

My mama was dreadful of learning to drive. Daddy thrived on having nice pickup trucks. One of my favorite was a canary yellow Ford F-100. He tried to interest Mama into getting behind the wheel and learning, but she would always decline. She finally shared with us even why Daddy would force us to learn, but was always calm and unforceful with her: Mama had dreamed that she died in a car accident. She said that it was so real that she knew that one day it would happen if she ever learned to drive.

How I remember that red one-room shack that was the neighborhood store owned by a white man who was kind to us. His big white house was in back of the store. He only sold snacks and sodas, but that was enough for our neighborhood children who would work for Daddy in the fields long enough to earn 15 cents so that they could by candy and an orange crush soda! My best friend's sister Becky was noted for working for about an hour, demanding pay, and then disappearing! I wanted to disappear with her to get out that beaming sun, but was not allowed. Yet I was so frail that I was never overworked, and many times Mama and Daddy would send me home to wash the dishes. That was wonderful to me! I hated the fields!

I couldn't for the life of me understand why my father and mother, who were older than the store owner, called him and every Caucasian neighbor Mr. or Ms. Even Caucasian children were addressed as such. "Yes suh" and "no suh," "yes ma'am" and "no ma'am" came from their lips when addressing this particular "lighter color."

Yet my family was loved and respected by them all, and as a result, household items, farm equipment, and clothing were given to us. We had absolutely no racial problems in our community. My sister Alice was even given a bird that she named Joe. The dogs got to him and ate him though, and my sister cried bitterly. We are all sad. Joe was the only bird that I was not afraid of!

The neighbors' younger son Allen would come and play with my younger siblings and me quite often. For some reason he paid special attention to me. We were about the same age. One day he asked me in an innocent, caring tone, "May I held you in my arms?" He extended his arms to me. I became frightened beyond measure! He was white!!! I told him "no" and ran home. He never came back to play again. I was sad that I ran him away from me and often dreamed of his return to extend his arms again. It never happened. Why was I so afraid?

His dad hired Mama and Daddy to work in his field, who gladly accepted, because they were at that time struggling in their own farming business, very much unlike Papa's masterful farming. Mama and my older sisters would also work as housekeepers for some of the Caucasian women in the neighborhood. They were terribly underpaid, but we needed any amount of money that could be attained. The neighborhood where Mama grew up was totally inhabited by black people. Daddy had moved her into an interracial neighborhood quite new to her, and she handled it by being herself—nice, sweet, kind, and loving. They all loved our family.

I knew that Mama was drawing strength from her own strong parents and siblings. She had fled my grandfather's farm and married into trouble. Yet she remained strong and very determined. Papa and Big Mama were stout against divorce and separation; yet Mama confided in me when I faced similar circumstances in my adulthood that they had indeed extended the invitation to her to go back home to them. She was adamant to not be a bother, and remained with my father who was very unfaithful. Yet he knew where home was and proved to my mama later on that God had gotten control of him also.

Her mother-in-law—my grandmother—could not stand the sight of her for some reason and plotted consistently to disgrace her and demote her character—actions that were very foreign to Mama who grew up sacredly adhering to privacy. Mary Massey Evans was the matriarch of the Evans family who lived just a few blocks up the road from us, close enough to mind our business. She loved me, but not my oldest sister! She would always tell untrue things about my sister, and as a result, she and my other older sister were almost imprisoned. If they went on a date, I was nominated to be in the back seat of the car. I hated it! So did my sisters!

Many times my sister in rebellion would sneak out of the house to meet with friends, but Daddy would always catch up with her and whip her with whatever he could get his hands on, even her baton that she expertly used as a majorette in high school.

I could not understand why my dad's mom led a chorus of in-laws who constantly exhibited hatred for my mom! Strangely, it was only the females of the family who did her so much wrong, and it caused me to shy away from them and my grandmother even though she adored me and would have done anything for me, especially after the accident that left me crippled and scarred. My mom, who was a very fair woman to look upon, even then was a tower of strength and saw the family through tragedy after tragedy. She never mistreated her mother-in-law. My mama was a superwoman and my hero.

MAMA MADE HER OWN BUTTER. I remember the old churn. She positioned it in front of a chair that she would sit in, and push and pull… She knew that the milk had turned into butter when it became too hard to continue to push and pull. The family enjoyed her buttermilk and cornbread combo, along with the cakes and pies she baked, using the butter made by her own hands.

Farm life was really not for me! I was afraid of all the animals, including the chickens and even the baby chicks that we called bitties! I was asked only once to go into the henhouse and gather eggs. After a hen flew out of the henhouse clucking and clacking loudly and pecking me on my head, I ran back into the house screaming! After they finished howling with laughter, Mama sent my sister out in my stead. They never sent me out there again! My sister was growing in envy as she realized more and more that the demand that was placed upon her was never imposed upon me. I was the little crippled weakling; she saw it as my being the favorite in the family.

One other time I was sent out to "slop the hogs." I told Daddy that I was scared! He just commanded me in that voice of authority that scared me more than the hogs did, and so I picked up the heavy bucket filled with left-overs and carried it to the hog pen. The moment the hogs saw me they started oinking and even hitting the sides of the wooden pen in an effort to make it to the slop! Their snouts were protruding between the boards! I was so afraid that I missed the trough and poured the slop on the ground outside of the pen! All the hogs broke out of the pen and ate as I ran as fast as my little crippled legs could carry me! Daddy had a fit, but he calmed down and put the hogs back into the security of the pen. He knew I was terrified and eventually blamed himself. He was just trying to get me to face my fears, but it wasn't working at all!

Then there were the days when the hogs were to be killed for food. Somehow they knew that one of them was to die that day! One could hear them squealing loudly very early in the morning, even before daybreak! It was such a heartbreaking sound that I would cover my head with my pillow. I stayed inside, refusing to view the hog's fate. I also refused to eat especially the souse made from the hogs' heads and the chitterlings, which were actually the hogs' intestines! Mama and Daddy managed to get me to eat a little bacon and pork chops because of my extreme anemic condition. I barely ate anything! I did like field peas if ketchup was on them, and butter beans. I was not about to eat that stuff they ate: birds, squirrels, rabbits, opossums, hog intestines… Yuck!!! Therefore, I remained puny and sickly, especially after the accident that changed my life and the lives of everyone on Tanyard Road.

The Curse

I was only four years old when tragedy struck my own life. Mama was blamed and openly criticized for my accident even though she was in the house with a very difficult last pregnancy and an epileptic son. She had left my older sisters and brothers in charge of me as they cleaned up the yard and started a fire to burn the debris. I spotted a slingshot and attempted to rescue it from the burning heap, and my wool skirt caught afire. The strong February breeze helped the flames to quickly consume my wool skirt and engulf my body as I fearfully ran down our long driveway. I did not know where I was going; I just ran!

Screams that came from my siblings and me echoed in the air and drew the attention of our neighbors. The nearest house was just yards away, and my best friend's sister Rudean, whom we affectionately called Dean, came running to the rescue. She caught me as I continued to run in a state of panic. She dipped my whole body into the barrel of water that Daddy had brought from town so that Mama didn't have to tote water from the spring that was about ¼ of a mile in the woods in back of our house. I overheard doctors saying that Dean's actions saved me from the flames. Years later this heroine of mine died of a severe heart attack.

I was alive, but didn't want to be because of the agony and pain. I spent many months trying to recover. I was not taken to the hospital when it first happened, because my parents had little money and no insurance. Our neighbor, nicknamed "Tutch", was a compassionate carpenter and our school bus driver. He adored me, stayed loyal to me, and made sure that I knew that I was still special. Under the country doctor's instructions, he built a table with a light attachment that was placed over my body as I lay in bed to "dry up my sores!"

I wasn't getting any better. The bed sheets were always soaked with my blood. When they would try to turn me over, my skin would come off. The light under the table made matters worse. My feet itched terribly, but I could not reach down to scratch them. Daddy prohibited Mama from scratching them for me, because she was pregnant. He didn't want her to "mark the baby." My sisters and brothers stayed away from me. They feared to touch me. So I would lay there daily crying and whimpering until a neighbor or visitor would come and rub my feet. The country doctor finally informed my parents that he could not do any more for me. He gave up. I was left to slowly die, but I did not die. That's when I saw the angel.

It was while I was under this "light treatment" that I saw an angel for the first time smiling reassuringly at me, and I slightly smiled back at him. I instinctively knew after seeing such a beautiful sight that I would be okay. After my experience with the angel, my Aunt Ruby came to Mama and Daddy and informed them that she had talked with someone she knew who told her about University Hospital in Jackson, Mississippi, where they accepted charity patients. I was rushed there and immediately given blood. The itching stopped. I was able to rest for a while. I was going to make it.

There at University Hospital I learned the true meaning of pain! Because I was a charity patient, I was treated as such. The assigned heavy-set nurse was extremely mean to me, and because we had learned false respect for Caucasians, my mom and dad endured her harsh roughness with me and never confronted her. When I would cry, she would snap at me, "Shut up!" Her commands to a four-year-old were mentally damaging: "Turn over!" "Be still!" She had no compassion for the pain I was enduring at such an early age. My four-year-old heart broke into pieces, for I had never been treated that way before. She would grab my arm and turn me over while changing bandages that hid my swollen, bleeding legs. One of my legs had to be treated specially, because the burns almost severed my main artery. They had to give me transfusions and performed multiple surgeries to save my leg and my life.

I remember the orderlies and nurses taking me into a room I now call hell! I cannot remember what they were doing, but the water hurt so badly. Constant skin grafts affected parts of me that were not burned. I hurt all over and even on the inside. That's when I just ignored the mean nurse and screamed as loudly as I could, calling for my mama who was not allowed to be there with me. I was surrounded by strangers, and that made it far worse to me than being at home with no one to rub my feet.

I shared the room with several others, including another black child about my age named Louis, who also was treated for third degree burns. All I saw was his damaged neck as he cried and moaned beside me as the nurse tortured him. At least I sustained burns on my lower parts, but his would show in spite of any clothing he would choose. When we were not in so much pain, we talked and encouraged each other to endure the nurse's maltreatment. I was amazed that he could carry on conversation with a four year old who talked as if she was twenty-one! He was the same. I often wonder what happened to him, or if he's a minister or some other special person! He was in pain, yet he never failed to cheer me up!

The hospital staff gave me six weeks of free treatments; then I was discharged back into the care of the country doctor who did not know what to do with me. Angels awaited my arrival and stood at attention as my family all gathered around the truck welcoming me home with guilt and sorrow on their countenances. I did not blame them; I knew that my intelligent spirit had been outwitted by my juvenile curiosity.

I had to learn to walk again after all the stress Mama endured to help me to walk for the first time at the age of eighteen months. Now I was again helpless like a baby. Yet I was no longer everyone's favorite as I was before the accident. All the people who before the accident came to hold me and listen to me talk (I was very tiny, but possessed great intelligence and an unusual ability to speak fluently,) disappeared. When they would visit my mom, they would not look at me. I was completely avoided. Now my baby sister, who was born in August of that year, was their new pet. I only had Mama and my best friend Rose. Rose was good to me and for me.

I felt like a freak, and people treated me as such. Even in those days Big Mama was careful to not spoil me too much. After all, they believed, that is why the accident took place. I stayed very close to Mama. The memory of the accident haunted me every single day of my young life. My thighs were black, grey, white and ugly!

I remember a song from back in the days when Mama and Daddy were still alive, and I was their struggling little cripple:

Someone who cares, someone who shares
All your troubles like no other can do;
He'll come down from the skies
And wipe the tears from your eyes.
You're His child, and He cares for you!

The author and singer of that song is also departed, yet the Lord saw fit to cause his words to continuously come alive and give me renewal of hope.

When I finally told my mama that the neighbor's shunning of me bothered me a lot, she revealed to me the reason for their withdrawal. An elderly neighbor, Addie Crisler, Mr. Tutch's wife, whom we affectionately called "Cudin (slang for Cousin) Ad", had warned them all that if they did not stop spoiling me, something bad would happen. It did. They actually thought they were doing me a favor by staying away.

It took me a while to forgive Cousin Addie Crisler for her words that I thought changed people's feelings for me, but now that I look back on it, I understand her passion completely. She babysat her grandchildren. Two of them were twin boys. I can remember the great commotion, the wails, and the screams as I sat in my mother's lap. She rushed with me to the door, and she screamed! One of the twins had been run over and killed by the mailman whose hurt face told all as he tried to explain how the child ran in front of the car, probably trying to get the mail for his ailing grandmother.

Cousin Addie took to the bed for a long time and was never the same again. It wasn't long at all that she died with a broken heart. One of the babies she loved and cherished died while in her care. That's why she told the others to not gloat over me. This was the first tragedy I was aware of, but later on my mama shared with me the trail of tragedies that took place prior to my birth.

After my accident I began to see visions of angels and strange creatures that I now know were demons. Only Rose believed me when I revealed my sightings, for she actually saw them as well. For some reason we named the demons we saw "gold bergs", whatever that is! The angels always looked like people with tattle-tell glows, and they always left me with a feeling of peace and assurance. The gold bergs were terrifying! They made me pray harder.

Rose was a year older than I, and she would come and help Mama with my brother and me as Mama tended to her last baby. Rose is very loving and considerate of everyone's feelings. Therefore, she made a point of assisting my mom during those dreadfully difficult times. I remember one occasion when Rose held my brother Melvin and rocked him in the red kiddie rocking chair I had gotten for Christmas; then all of a sudden Melvin had an epileptic seizure. Rose and I both panicked, but Mama handled him very tenderly with tears in her eyes until the spirit let go.

According to Mama's in-laws, she was under a curse for revealing to them that her sister-in-law's husband had made advances toward her. She was accused of making it all up to break up the family. I knew that Mama somewhat wondered if their "revelations" of curses were true, or that all of this was happening because she eloped.

My grandmother, Mary Massey Evans, was a mixture of Caucasian and African American, and my grandfather Clifton (Papa Cliff) was very dark. Therefore there was a strange mixture of color in Daddy's family of eleven siblings. My dad had four beautiful sisters, and two of them were very cunning! The oldest of them, Mary Ella, had flaming red hair and freckles. We loved her a lot, especially when she would have her parties at her cafe and invite us once a year, usually on the Fourth of July, to eat barbequed goat. The other three had cold black hair and very fair skin.

Daddy and his older brothers Wilmer (Uncle Snag), Jim, and Pete were "high yellow" with freckles. Daddy was nicknamed "Red" because his color resembled more of the color red than yellow and because his temper was flaming red. His hair was also red. The other brothers, Earl and Walter, were dark skinned like my grandfather whom I had never met. There was also Eddie nicknamed "Teenie", an older brother born before Papa Cliff married Mom Mary. I never really saw much of him. Yet my dad often spoke very fondly of his big brother.

Tragedy was definitely in this family. Papa Cliff died before I was born; so did my Uncle Walter. They both died in truck accidents. Uncle Jim was to follow much later while helping someone out of a ditch. A large logging truck sped along and the driver saw him too late. He couldn't stop. The truck pinned him between it and the truck he was assisting, severing his body. He lived for one hour afterward.

Daddy's baby sister Ruby was beautiful, but was marred by her husband's wrath. He shot her chin off; then turned the gun on himself. She lived, but never spoke openly about the tragedy. Men still loved her! Her scars did not matter to them!

Aunt Mamie Lee died after having her baby boy, who is the same age as I, leaving several children orphaned, for her husband had also passed; yet the children all have found Christ. Daddy and the other surviving brothers, especially Uncle Earl, made sure that her children were seen about.

Daddy was a "rolling stone", and he had been sighted on many occasions. This made Mama furious, but she refused to go back home even though Papa opened the door for her on many occasions. His Pharisaical stand on divorce could not deter him from hating to see her go through so much! Yet he never mistreated Daddy, nor did he even scold him for his behavior. Papa and Big Mama still treated him with the same level of respect and dignity as they had previously, never making a scene. Their children's business was not theirs anymore. They only offered advice when asked. Mama and Daddy practiced this same policy when their offspring left the nest. So do I.

My oldest brother, Carls Edward, (whom we, for some reason unknown to me, called "Boo"), was lively and giddy until the day he spotted Daddy's hunting shotgun hanging on the way and decided to play with it. I was in the back room watching as he aimed the gun away from me and imagined that he saw game. "Hey, there goes a rabbit!" he shouted and pulled the trigger. To his startling surprise and mine, there was a bullet in the old shot gun. It blew a large hole into the bedroom wall and barely missed Mama in the kitchen as it exited the outer wall. Mama screamed her favorite word, "Sh..!" Then she ran into the bedroom where we were still standing in a shocked state. She yelled at him so terribly till I really felt sorry for my brother.

He didn't mean to do it. Yet when Daddy came home from the woods, my brother was cussed out so badly that he went into a depression that he never came out of. We all were silent until Mama made a joke of it, as she always would to lighten the atmosphere. She mocked the sound of the bullet as it went past her ear, "Whoosh!" and began to laugh. We all joined into the chorus of laughter, but Boo remained silent and withdrawn. The tragedy was not the accident; the tragedy was my brother's withdrawal. His spirit died that day.

The sorrows in my own life multiplied when I had to be enrolled into public school. I was then extremely timid and withdrawn, and had hid behind Mama ever since the fire ravaged my body and mind; yet Mama knew that she had to lengthen her apron strings and allow me to grow and develop. It broke her heart to dress me and put my tiny hand into the hand of my older sisters who led their teary little sister to the bus.

I was not afraid at first, because Mr. Tutch was the bus driver, and he greeted me at the door of the bus with a big smile. I only became stricken with fear when we drove up to the big place where I had never been before, and Mr. Tutch had to escort me off the bus. Then he too let go. That's when I pitched a fit and would not stop crying very loudly in spite of his reassuring words. I wanted to go back home to Mama, but this was the day of transition for me. My life would never be the same again.

Another man who was extremely Christian was "Cud'n" (Cousin) Manuel Ford, who lived up the road apiece. Faithful to God and the church, he and his sweet wife Irene, along with Mr. Tutch, made sure that my mama and daddy knew that they were never alone in their struggles.

Cud'n Manuel was a faithful deacon who loved to sing in the senior choir at New Pisgah Missionary Baptist Church deep off in the woods of Copiah County. His favorite song that was even sung at his funeral was "Life's Railway to Heaven." I can still hear his calm, serene bass voice singing,

"Life is like a mountain railroad with an engineer that's brave;
We must make the run successful from the cradle to the grave;
Watch the curves, the fills, the tunnels; never falter, never fail;
Keep your hand upon the throttle, and your eyes upon the rail."

Manuel Ford passed away a short while after burying his wife. As he sat at the wooden heater, his heart gave way to death. One of his feet was fastened to the heater and blackened when he was found. I believed that was the only burn he would ever again receive; I was certain that he was in heaven with his wife Irene. I loved and respected him so much! I grieved his passing, because I had lost one of the few who didn't look funny and turn away at the sight of me.

I felt the same about Mr. Tutch, who had to endure cussing and teasing from some of the neighboring children who rode the bus to school. They would run and play on the bus in spite of his warnings. One day I stood up and told them all, "You ought to respect that man!" I scared myself! I could not believe that a puny little girl like me had just stood up to older and bigger children! A hush went over the whole bus; then the silence was broken by two of the older children. "You shut up, Respect!" They laughed at me and teased me from that time forward, calling me "Respect." Rose was my only friend. She told me to just ignore them. It was hard! I never told Mama how badly Mr. Tutch and I were being teased. I attribute their bad behavior to growing up without a father.

I had so much overflowing respect for that man who had helped to save my life. As far as I was concerned, he was one of the angels! I was dear to him, and he was very dear to me! Many times he defended me against those school bus bullies as they made fun of my clothes, my scrawny body, my less than stylish hairdos, and my legs.

Maybe that's why I was not defended by my sisters and brothers the first time Mama allowed me to walk to a faraway corner store with the older children. I looked like a three-year-old, though I was six. Therefore, I had a hard time keeping up with them, but Mama made them promise to take care of me. Every now and then one of them would turn around and yell at me, "come on, Slow-poke!" I would then hear one of them whisper,

"I wish we had left her at home." Tears would well up in my eyes, but I was determined to go the distance.

We had to go through pastures to make our journey shorter, for the store was about 3½ miles from our house. The shortcut we took made it only about two miles away. All was well until we made it to a certain pasture full of big, fierce-looking bulls! A shush came over everybody as the oldest of our traveling group told us to be as quiet as possible. Each child crossed the bob-wire fence cautiously and proceeded to the other side. I was the last one to cross over.

The bulls fastened their eyes on me, and suddenly one of them charged after me. The others, safely on the other side, shouted to me, "Run, Maxine!" I ran as fast as my little, scarred legs could take me and actually outran the bull! My red sweater became snared by the bob wire and it took a minute to loose myself, and I tore it in the effort. All were gone ahead, and I couldn't yell out for anyone to wait on me. Rose's sister Becky grabbed me and pulled me over the barbed wire fence as fast as she could, scarring one of my legs on the bob wire. I escaped the bull, but not the jeers and ogles from the entourage that really wished I had stayed home. They said it was the red sweater I was wearing that had attracted the bulls. I felt that it was more.

Because I felt so alone and abandoned, it was even harder for me to adjust to public school. All the children looked at me and my legs as if they had seen a monkey or something, and they would snicker and whisper among themselves. I cried even harder and withdrew to the corners of the room every day. First grade was so difficult for me, because for the first time in my life I had to stay away from Mama all day. Oh how I wished for her reassuring looks as I sat at the tiny desk and watched the other kids laugh at me.

Mrs. Evans (no relation to me) was my first teacher who felt so very sorry for me; yet she could do nothing to console me. She would send for my older sister, Hattie Rean, who would come and take me to the little corner store adjacent to the school, buy me cookies, and take me back to the classroom. The first time she did this was disastrous. I put the bag of cookies in the book section under the seat of my desk, and they soon disappeared. I cried again, and my sister promised me that she would buy me more.

The snickers from the other children only made me feel more like a freak, so Mrs. Evans soon gave up and referred me to another first grade teacher—Mrs. Bartley, who was sympathetic, but firm and big for a woman. She commanded me to stop crying with a tone of voice that was foreign to Mrs. Evans, who was soft spoken. I hushed! She then would take me into her arms and hold me in a way that let me know that I was safe. I loved her so much, and Mama stopped worrying about me.

It was Mrs. Bartley's firm love that brought out gifts that were secretly hidden within me. Under her caring instructions, I learned just how intelligent I really was and began to speak publicly. I also learned to write cursively in first grade—a great accomplishment for a black child in that day. She, with my mama's permission, enrolled me into the 4-H club, where I learned to stand poised before an audience and recite poems and speeches. Fear gripped me every time I was to speak at an assembly, and I would tremble so badly that the students would laugh. I wanted to run off the stage, but Mrs. Bartley would be standing right there to make sure that I did not run from my making! Soon I mastered the crowd of cruelty and was able to make long speeches without fear, even making gestures with my mouth and tiny body that drew a different type of laughter from them! They approved! They showed it with thunderous applause!

My teacher gleamed with pride! Sometimes I would overhear her talking to other teachers and the principle about me and would get quiet when she noticed my attention. I never really heard all they were saying; all I know is that after her conversations about me, these people would place me into more programs and clubs!

Mrs. Bartley never allowed my self-pity to deter her from firmly guiding me onto the road of my destiny. She saw in me what I could not see in myself and made sure that everyone else respected me for it. Even after I was promoted to second grade, Mrs. Bartley kept an eye open for me. I discovered that her infatuation with me gained both admirers and critics. Jealous classmates made sure that I was miserable everyday by calling me "teacher's pet", burnt legs, freak, cry-baby, and more!

I just wanted to be left alone. I had no friends at school, and Rose was in the next grade. My older brother Robert, who wailed on his first day of third grade, was no help at all. I felt consoled that someone else cried too until I was told the reason for his sobbing—he had the meanest teacher in the school, Mrs. Williams! Everybody dreaded her class and would cringe as she would walk down the hall very authoritatively, looking like the wicked witch from "The Wizard of Oz." We actually used to call her that! Yet everybody in elementary school had to take music lessons from "the witch!" Robert flunked third grade.

We all laughed so hard at Robert, because he had to be in Mrs. Williams' class twice! Therefore, he was only one grade ahead of me, and I could spot Rose and him at times. It was then that I loosened up and won a friend—Linda April Catchings. Linda was smart, gifted, cute, and very dark. The children picked at her about her dark skin and at me about my scars. Boys would see us coming and shout, "Burnt legs and black legs!" Their laughter made us so angry, but we had each other to comfort, and it made all the difference with me. I was no longer the only "freak" in the school. Of course, there was nothing wrong with Linda's color. She was beautiful to me, but because she was with me, her color was highlighted in the eyes of the other school children who taunted me daily. Yet she remained faithful to our friendship and scolded those who teased me.

Linda could draw and taught me to do so. Yet my sketches could not compete with hers. She drew paper dolls and clothes for them. The other girls in the class would play with hers, but not with mine. It was okay. I had so many other skills that it really didn't matter that I would not really master this one in the eyes of the children. Yet I won first place for a painting of a little girl reaching for a rose at my third grade 4-H club contest. I took it home with pride and Mama made it a wall display in our living room.

After my third grade year in school, I found myself alone again. Linda's family moved away, and I didn't seem to fit in with any of the other clicks. Therefore, I began to withdraw again. I would just do my work, write poems, and draw images. Sometimes I tried to be part of the click, but with no success. Even the "cool girls" tried at times to draft me in, and they even gave me a pet name "Candy", but it didn't last. I was, in every sense of the word, a geek! I was very old fashioned and out of touch with the townspeople, simply because I was isolated from them all on Tanyard Road amid only those who were just like me.

I knew I had been set apart from everyone else, but it wasn't because of my injuries. I knew deep inside that I was simply different. I just wanted to be like everyone else. Yet I wasn't like everyone else, and never would be.

Every now and then the teachers would allow students to have parties within the classroom. All desks would be pushed to the sides and corners of the rooms, the teacher would play "safe" music on the record player, and the students would dance. I could not dance. I would stand in corners with the desks and chairs, espying one boy with whom I had a big crush until one day I was pulled out to the dance floor by one of my female classmates. I tried to dance like them, but I quickly realized that I was the center of laughter! I had two left feet! I was only nine years old, had the body of a six year old, and had the moves of a toddler! I would always be glad when the bell rang for us to board the bus and go home.

I soon found refuge at Free People Missionary Baptist Church. It was at Free People that I began to really understand that God had hand-picked me for something very special. I soon was old enough to join the junior choir, but nobody could hear my quiet, shy voice. Then there was the inspirational choir, where I was finally asked to lead a song. Of course, my first response was an emphatic fearful NO! Yet I was talked into it, and my tenure in singing began when I was 12.

The loving pastor, Reverend P. J. Hopkins, made sure that I knew that God had handpicked me! I remember his tearful words from the pulpit after I had led a song that ignited his heart, "Maxine, God has called you for something very special. You are going to be a great lady! Mark my words for it: Maxine is going to be a great lady!" The assembly became ghostly quiet as the congregation spied me with a serene sense of admiration. I was encouraged, to say the least! They all celebrated me, and it helped me to forget the loneliness I felt.

I cherished the times when I went to Baptist Training Union meetings with Pastor Hopkins. BTU's were boring but instrumental in my inner Christian growth and development, and these meetings brought out the gifts I had suppressed and the knowledge that everybody is somebody in Christ. I also had friends at these meetings, especially Magnolia Wade, my cousin, and her younger sister, who were then being kept by their grandmother. She and I would co-lead songs in the small makeshift choir; my favorite that I sang with her was "Move to the Sky". I never imagined that Magnolia would become the famous anchorwoman Maggie Wade Dixon who is now a long-time anchor for WLBT News. I could not be more proud of my cousin and friend! We loved being with each other! We both grew up and went our separate ways; yet the fondness is still very present. She is such a wonderful person filled with integrity.

I was a good student in school, but was obsessed with loving and being loved. I was a broken doll who desperately wanted someone to look past my brokenness and scars and call me beautiful. That was an almost fatal mistake.

Seventh grade made up for the aloneness I had endured. I fell in love—twice! Over the summer before my transition into middle school I met Rose's cousin Charlie Haynes Jr., who gave me my first kiss. I fell deeply in love with this tall, dark, slender, not so handsome, and big-eared boy who was a year older than me. He made me feel pretty in spite of my scars. He never acted as if he saw them. We would just walk, talk, and innocently kiss. I felt like I was in heaven whenever he was around. The summers he would visit from that time forward were never long enough, and I would cry bitterly when he would have to go back home to New Orleans. Rose would try to console me, but to no avail. My heart ached for the attention I only received during those hot summer months!

I soon learned that Charlie was there to open me up, to show me that my scars don't matter to everyone. I wanted him to be the man I would marry, but he was not in my life to stay, but rather to let me know that someone would love me even because of the scars.

When I went into seventh grade I met someone else who "rocked my world!" A slender good-looking athlete came into my life suddenly after failing a couple of grades! He ended up in the classes with me, and again I thought I had fallen in love. Is it possible to love two guys at the same time?

Now that I look back on it, I really feel strongly that I was in love with the attention. This one whom I will call Tony also made me feel beautiful, but he also made other girls feel the same way! I seemed to have been his special choice, but I soon learned that at our age, what we termed as love is not really to be taken very seriously. If I had just walked away when I first realized that I was not his only love, I would have spared myself much grief. I held on to his masculine demeanor, fully aware that I was headed for a whole lot of trouble!

Yet the first months of knowing Tony were innocent, sweet, and fulfilling. He walked me to class every day and stayed with me at the door until the bell rang to come in and take a seat. I could tell that teachers didn't like this relationship, but I cherished it. I would meet him at ball games and socials, and loved to see eyes full of envy as they gazed at us!

When I was 13, it was time to say goodbye to Big Mama. Mama received the word late one evening to hurry to her childhood home. Mama took her younger children, including me, with her. Of course, Daddy accompanied her. Colon cancer had taken its toll on Big Mama as her weakening body lay on her clean white linen in the bed we were not allowed to touch. Doctors were no longer being called. They only sat at her bedside, awaiting the inevitable.

I was only allowed to peek in on her for a little while; then my sister, brother, and I were ushered on to the porch where we sat in the swing, accompanied by Papa, the men of the family and my dad. It was so dark that we could barely see one another, but we did not dare go back into the house where my mother and some of her sisters had gathered, for Big Mama was groaning in pain. I could hear her crying in a very weak voice, "Come, and get me, Rosie!" I wondered who Rosie was; someone on the porch answered my inquiring thoughts—Rosie was Big Mama's best friend who had died years before.

At that very moment, Papa asked the question, "Who is that woman?" I looked out and saw her! A woman of average height and build with a white apron tied around her waist (it was too dark for me to see the color of her other clothing) was walking up the path; then she suddenly disappeared. The news came to us from the bedroom at that very moment that Big Mama had passed. Daddy was then ready to disappear! He had seen the woman also! He tried to be patient for Mama's sake, but soon we were in the car traveling back down the path towards home.

I discovered later that Daddy was terrified of spirits. Mama was the one who could see them; yet every now and then Daddy would catch a glimpse of one and quickly deny it. His terrified countenance told off on him though. He never forgot the sighting of that woman at the very instant that Big Mama breathed deeply for the last time, and neither did I.

That same year, my cousin talked Mama into letting me go with her to my first party. I was not on the invitation list; yet she assured Mama and me that it would be fine for me to go. Immediately after we arrived, she disappeared, and I was left alone in the yard. I found out too late that uninvited guests were not allowed inside.

The boy that I was so very fond of, who paid so much attention to me at school, and who told me that he loved me, was there with another girl. When he saw me, he rolled his eyes in anger that I was there and turned away. I was so upset that I wanted to go home, but I could not find my cousin. An older boy drove up and asked me if I would like to go for a ride. I reluctantly consented after he told me that it would be just a quick ride. He assisted me to the car, opened the door for me, and we drove to a deserted wooded area. I knew I was in trouble and began to cry when he opened the glove compartment and a gun almost fell out of it. He took it and something in a packet that I now know was a condom. I fearfully, emotionally lost my virginity that night.

When he had finished, he drove me back to the street where the party was being held and stopped in front of the driveway. Still weeping, I exited the car, and he immediately sped off. When the boy I thought loved me saw this, he ran over to me and slapped me so hard that I actually saw stars! I wept loudly. The young hostess of the party who was my age and in my classroom came to the door and said something. I knew that she was fussing, but I could not hear a word. She then slammed the door. It was final to me. I would never fit in to this fast crowd. I was glad that door shut in my face!

My cousin had heard about what had taken place with the boy and appeared to take me home. She fixed my clothes and hair and cautioned me to tell no one, especially Mama. She convinced me that no one would believe that it was rape, since I willingly got into his car. It made sense to my 13-year-old logic; so I tried to bury the very memory of the entire night. We lived in a small town; word would get around. I knew my rapist, and my rapist knew me.

I withdrew from everyone after that and refused to leave the house except for school and work in the fields. Mama sensed that something was wrong, but when she asked me, I just said that I was okay. Soon she stopped asking.

I did manage to make friends again, but with the ones who were also tagged as freaks! Two of my favorite were sisters—Maggie and Zerra Bridges—a midget and a giant! Everyone else was afraid of them! So they became my body guards! I loved it!

I also gained the friendship of Lucille Lilly, who was always getting me into trouble, but I loved her. We were drawn to each other for some reason that I was unaware of until after high school and college, I received the news that she had passed away from complications of sickle cell anemia. Then I understood the attachment.

Tony again took special interest in me as I developed and began to capture the attention of other boys. My fondest memory of being with him was after a football game. A fight had erupted during half time when we walked to the concession stand. Tony protectively steered me away from the confusion. Then a car pulled up beside us, and two drunken older boys eyed me. The driver said to Tony, "That's a good-looking girl you have with you!" For the first time I heard fear in Tony's voice as he let out a shaky laughter. Then the one in the passenger seat, as his head bobbed from the alcohol, opened the glove compartment and reached for a big gun that was very visible. As Tony embraced me and backed me away, the driver patted the passenger's hand and said, "Naw, not that." They then spun away in that old Chevy. I instinctively knew that Tony was aware of the fact that these boys were dangerous, and it frightened me greatly.

From that time forward, Tony kept me very close to him! After the game when it began to drizzle, he borrowed an umbrella from a friend and walked with me, shielding me from the raindrops. The little corner store where my sister had bought me cookies in first grade was our destination. He wanted to buy cookies for me! No boy had ever bought me anything! I was blown away!

We walked slowly in the rain soaking in every moment we had with each other, full of gratitude that we had not become casualties that evening! Ironically, the store owner played the song, "Walking in the rain with the one I love: feel so fine!" When he bought the cookies, he looked lovingly at me and said, "Sweets for a sweet." Wow! We kissed each other somewhat innocently until it was time for my ride to take me home to the parents who would have killed me if they had known that I was kissing a boy! Hey, we were not even allowed to date until we were seventeen!

The Pedophile

One of my favorite people who lived on Tanyard Road had a dark secret. He was seemingly nice and fun-loving! His gentle, goofy nature never betrayed that other side of him from which we should have steered away. Even if we had told what he was doing, I don't think we would have been believed. Everybody loved him!

He introduced the children on Tanyard Road to gin; then took them on rides with him in that old squeaking pickup truck. There in that truck he would molest some of them. The older children never said a word about it, but I always smelled the odor of the liquor. I was by nature very quiet, and I never told. Whether my older sisters were meddled with or not is yet to be revealed.

This went on for a long time until my baby sister Ann and I were old enough to "ride" with him. He never molested me. I'm thinking that it was because of my scars, and also because he knew that I had a keen sense of right and wrong. I would not even drink the gin. My sister sat in the middle of the only seat of the old truck, and I sat by the door. According to him, her seating was to keep her from accidentally falling out, because she was only about 5 or 6 at the time. He stopped and got out of the truck for something that escapes my memory; and while he was out, Ann told me that he was feeling on her. That's when my protective big-sister instincts took over. I told her to trade places with me. I sat by him. It was then over. He, looking very puzzled at the switch in seating, took us back home and never tried it again in my presence.

Ann later in life told me that he had done it to her again while they were alone. She bore all the symptoms of molestation, and I never doubted her story. While I was away performing in high school choral competitions, she finally told Mama what was happening. She confided in me later that Mama had instructed her to be quiet about it, because certain people would not believe her, but would rather become angry and mistreat her as she had been mistreated. Ann did as she was instructed, but held it against Mama for the rest of her life.

The news came in later years that our local pedophile had been killed in a freak accident. He was using that same truck to pull another man's truck out of a ditch when a third truck turned the curve fiercely and crashed into his truck. The impact pinned him between the two trucks and disfigured him. I was told that body parts were scattered everywhere. Only his head and torso remained, and he lived for about an hour after that awful incident.

My baby brother Melvin sobbed bitterly over the news. Ann and I laughed about it! My heart was very cold by that time, and I just didn't care what happened to a pedophile! Melvin became very angry with us and threatened us if we didn't stop laughing. We realized the impact our senseless actions had on him and apologized over and over again. Yet the anger in him grew into rage. We thought that maybe the bloody lump on his head after falling off my uncle's truck years before had affected him after all, even though the doctor had said that he was alright. He was becoming almost murderous. I later found out that the man had introduced him also to alcohol and whatever else! We became more and more afraid of my baby brother. His spirit had died.

My grandmother died in 1972 from a massive stroke that first disabled her from speaking, but not from using her eyes to express how she felt especially about Mama. Just before she passed daddy, mama, Ann, Melvin and I went to visit her. If looks could kill, my mama would have died right then and there! Yet my hero mom ignored her ogles and continued to clean and cook for her until her death. Mama was my hero!

As we left her house and headed back home, Ann and I decided to walk until as we exited the house a black cat jumped out at Daddy! We all, except Daddy, screamed. Daddy was startled, but recomposed himself as the cat ran away. I knew that it was weird and considered it as a sign of something bad about to happen. The next day Mama Mary passed away. Black cats have always been symbols of witchcraft. Ann and I wondered among ourselves why the cat leaped out towards Daddy.

I went off to college after graduation from high school and learned that I could not trust myself. I made good grades, but could have done better. I was a Dean's List student and could have very easily made the President's List. I did not want to. I did not care. College was just something else to do to get away from that hard farm work.

My stay in college lasted for two years; I grew weary of it, and promising to go back after taking a short break, I went home to find a job as a business administrator. I received a call from Alcorn State University to come there and work with the Department of Industrial Education. Thus I had my first official job. I also adopted studies on my own terms while at Alcorn State.

Daddy was so proud of me that he bought me a brand new Ford Torino for the lengthy commute. Lorman, Mississippi was about 60 miles from my home; so daily I drove 120 miles round trip to work and school. This proved to be very strenuous! I had to get up very early in the morning to make it to the school by 7 o'clock, and I often ran late! Therefore, to make up the time, I drove in excess of 80-90 mph.

On one particular morning I actually fell asleep behind the wheel and heard a man's voice shout my name, MAXINE! My eyes popped open, and I realized that I was headed for an extremely deep ditch with water in it! If I had fallen into it, I would probably have not been found for days! Buzzards would have had to indicate where I was to the few commuters who traveled on that lonely stretch of highway. I hit the brakes as hard as I could and screamed JESUS!!! The car went into a spin, skidding as it twirled on the narrow stretch of highway 27, and suddenly stopped just before plummeting into the deep ravine!

Trembling all over, I exited my car to regain my composure. That's when I saw the miracle! Sand had heaped up in front of all four tires on the highway that was totally paved! The sand had stopped the car from skidding into the ravine! I searched for evidence of how the sand could have appeared, but there was none. Who was the man who called my name?

I climbed back into my car, carefully drove at a much lower speed, and was delighted to see Highway 61 which would take me to Alcorn. I was alive! How?!

I shared the incidence with my supervisor, who was the head of the department; and he immediately went to work to find a place for me to stay that would be closer to the University. A couple in Fayette, a small town only a few miles from Alcorn, agreed to allow me to live with them during the week, and by my own choice, to travel to home on weekends. I was extremely shy and introverted and really did not desire to live with anyone other than my own family; but the thought of the near fatal accident convinced me to stay.

I was alone and lonely and soon began to attract male students who were the same age as I. My supervisor did not want me to fraternize with them, but I was too young to socialize with the crowd that he was accustomed to being with. He also was a Church of God in Christ minister, and I was a Baptist and a big sinner! He did his best to get me into church there, but my home church was the only one that still interested me.

One weekend afternoon as I slept on the sofa at my parents' home I heard the door open, and a dark tall figure walked over to me and did something to me as I lay there unable to move. I felt this strange very pleasant sensation that I had never felt before in my life! It then arose and walked back out the door. I could move again, but for some reason I didn't. I just kept this to myself for a long time.

After that I fell in love with a college student. I wished I hadn't! There were many males that were attracted to me, but only one had my eyes, my ears, my mind, and my heart! He had all of me! I began to be very nauseated and moody. One trip to the doctor shattered my heart. I was pregnant. He wanted me to have an abortion. The doctor offered me a pill that would "take care of it right away!" I turned it down, turned in my resignation at work, and went home to my mother and father.

I dreaded telling them, but I finally became brave enough to talk to my mom. Her temper hit the ceiling! I was the first one to disgrace the family that way, and she was extremely disappointed with me. I was also very disappointed with myself. I needed comfort and encouragement, but didn't find any that night…or the next…or the next!

When Daddy finally came home late that night, she shouted the news to him, "Your daughter is expecting!!!" "Expecting what?" He looked so puzzled until she clarified it to him, "A BABY!!!" In a very careless voice, he let her know that he was not surprised. He knew all the time that I had become sexually active, but never said a word. Even then he didn't mistreat me; he just didn't talk about it at all.

Mama was the mean one! She refused to walk beside me in public. When we went to church, she told me to walk behind her, not beside her. She pretended in stores to not know me. That hurt! Yet I never responded to it, because I knew I had disgraced the family. I cried in private.

My baby sister, who was tagged as the bad girl of the family, because she was always being caught in some kind of mischief, rejoiced at the news! She laughed and teased me about it! "Miss Goody Two-shoes is pregnant!!!" Mama would tell her to stop, but she just kept going on and on with it! I couldn't even respond. She was right. I was the one who was supposed to make everyone proud; yet I am the one who opened the door to reproach.

One sunny Sunday afternoon Mama wanted ice cream. I gladly drove her to the ice cream factory in town, and as I sat there waiting baby's daddy drove up and began flirting with some of the girls with whom I went to high school. I was totally hurt! I had not seen nor heard from him at all since a day before I left the college campus; then when I see him again, he's flirting with someone else, or so I thought! Mama saw my expression, and she asked me, "Is it him?" I replied in a very low tone, "Yes ma'am." He spotted me and walked over to the car. He very casually said hey to me and asked how I was doing. I told him that I was okay, but I wasn't. I would not even look at him! He said, "Okay, see you later." He walked away, and I gladly pulled off for home. Mama treated me more kindly after that. She knew how hurt I was.

The pregnancy was very painful and difficult. I couldn't use the bathroom on my own. I remember the doctor's orders to Mama to give me enemas! It didn't help though. Something was wrong. They said I almost died! The doctors warned me that she should be my only child, or the next one would kill me.

My first-born was overlaid. My oldest sister said she was a blue baby. She also said she was born with a veil. I didn't pay any attention to it, because I really didn't understand the significance of it. My 7 pound, 8½ ounce first-born was beautiful! To my relief, Mama, Daddy, and the entire family adored her! It was truly love at first sight!

I stayed in the hospital with her for about three days, then released. Mama and Daddy loaned me their bedroom for a while, because so many people were coming to see the baby. Their bedroom was immediately adjacent to the living room. She wouldn't stop crying! I insisted on being the mommy, in spite of my Mama's pleas with me to help. I began to cry soon, because she persisted in wailing. I prayed to God to help me with her. I then heard a voice, "Turn her this way." I instinctively knew what the voice meant and turned her toward the wall where Mama had hung a picture of Jesus! She immediately stopped crying, and I never had that problem with her again.

When Kim was about three months old, just before Christmas, I had let myself go so badly that my mom asked my sister to take me in because she couldn't handle it anymore. Of course, I was hurt by it, but I wasn't working or anything! I was a depressed young woman with a baby whom Mama adored, but she couldn't stand to see me waste away. She didn't mind the baby; she didn't want me around anymore.

Suddenly there was a knock on my sister's door. Baby's daddy stood there when I opened it. I was alone with my baby. My sister Rean had contacted him and made him feel ashamed for the abandonment. I was very quiet and casual with him. He asked to see the baby. I went into the bedroom where she lay, cuddled her in my arms, and took her to see her daddy for the first time. He held her briefly, smiled, and left us again. This time he remained invisible for almost 30 years.

His walking away again broke my spirit completely. I felt worthless as a woman and as a human being. I began to date again, but with the vilest, most worthless men I knew. I didn't feel that I could do any better.

Love never really dies; it just seems to go into a coma until someone worthy awakens it.

I also began to drink heavily and visit club spots. I didn't care whether I lived or died, so even those lowly honky tonks didn't frighten me. Bullets many times would fly over my head, and I would just laugh. Several times I was threatened with guns and knives by men who thought that I loved them, but found me with someone else sometimes the same nights that I would have just been with them! Again I would just laugh! I quickly gained the reputation of being crazy, and men began to back away. So the bottle became my man.

I soon became so indulged with strong drinks that I found myself drinking every morning before driving to work. I felt that I was trained at it, for I knew just how much it would take to "make me feel better." I praise God now that I didn't kill myself and others who were doing the same as we carpooled to Jackson from Crystal Springs. I needed help.

Most people did not know that I had become addicted to alcohol, and even my mom missed the signs. I would come home and go into laughing fits and clowned around, but I had developed that pattern even before I began to drink. So she did not catch on to it in the beginning, but Daddy did and never spoke about it. He just kept an extra eye open for me so that I would not be allowed to self-destruct.

When Kim was almost a year old, Daddy bought another house and had it moved a few yards further down the road to the very spot where my best friend's house once stood, but was torn down. Mama had allowed me to move back in with them, and she kept Kim for me for a season even when I was out binge drinking. That is when I began to have definite encounters with God. I had begun to recover.

Trophy Wife

On a beautiful Sunday morning in May as we dutifully prepared for church service I heard a song on WOKJ radio, the only station at that time that aired black Gospel, yet on Sundays only. This song shook me. "God still loves you!" The lyrics permeated the atmosphere to the degree that my brother Melvin jumped out of the bed he had made as his sanctuary to avoid going to church! He cried out, "Maxine! Do you hear that song?!"I shouted, "YES!!!" We both vowed to give our lives to Christ that morning. He gladly attended church service that day a few more Sundays afterwards.

A few months later my brother reneged on his promise and began to drink more heavily than ever before. He moved into the old house, and distanced himself from the family. On one particular instance he showed up at the new dwelling yelling and slamming doors. His noise awakened Kim, and I scolded him. He yelled back, and I threatened him with the hot iron I was using. He was not riled at all! He walked up to me while I still held the heated iron and dared me to use it. That was not my brother I was beholding! Something had him, and that something frightened me greatly! I backed away from him and saw about Kim. He left...he left the house and my heart.

After my brother's separation from me, I repeatedly dreamed about hell. One particular dream caused me to really examine myself—I was walking right into the bottomless pit of hell and could not stop! One foot was over the hole when I awakened from the dream in tears and prayers for repentance.

I then began to dream of joining what we then called the sanctified church—the very type of church that I once laughed about and avoided. I would see the women walking down the streets of our town without makeup or jewelry, but rather with their long ankle-length dresses, closed in shoes, nape- and elbow-covered blouses, and prayer cloths draped over their heads; and I vowed that I would never be one of them! I loved my skin-tight pants, afro hairdo, and jewelry! So being among then was the last thing I wanted! Yet I was being drawn out of the water like a fish on a hook!

I prayed at the Baptist church so intensely that the deacons peered at me curiously and began to whisper. That's when the congregations I had grown to know and love began to withdraw from me. I knew I had to leave and cried bitterly because of it. I heard then a voice that said, "Contact Deacon Gray." That was another thing that I did not want to do! My sister had contact information on him. Because of scandals, she had recently left the church that he still attended.

When I told her of my dreams and visions, she immediately called him and arranged a meeting. Yet before meeting with him, she took me to the church that she had joined, Greater Bethlehem Temple, and there I was immediately baptized in Jesus Name. Change had taken me over, and it was as if I had no control of my life anymore! I was being ushered into a new realm with God; and, though I was afraid, I knew it was God.

I met with him at the church he attended in Jackson, Mississippi. I meant to only stay for a few minutes, and then go back to Crystal Springs. Yet the pastor's message was so penetrating that I remained there in literal tears! He was revealing my entire life before everyone! I felt betrayed by Deacon Gray; I was sure that he had told his pastor about my history. He had not! It was God. The pastor made altar call, and I just sat there in the back of the church crying. A young very devout woman, Sister Annie Mae Epps, came and asked me if I wanted prayer. She took me by the hand and ushered me to the front of the church.

Whispers went all over the church! He then said to the congregation, "Leave her alone! She wants to be saved!" What that was all about, I don't know; yet I was treated with kindness and respect after his bold proclamation. I didn't understand why most of the members were cold and distant from me until later on. They knew who's sister I was! My sister had accused the pastor of something horrible! That's why she had left the church; yet there I was weeping on the altar! I felt that I was betraying her by being there, but she was the one who contacted Deacon Gray on my behalf.

That same day I became a member. I shared it with my sister who immediately became irate! She couldn't believe that I had joined that church! She then revealed her experience to me. I asked her why she had not shared this before I met with Deacon Gray. She said she didn't want to discourage me from seeking for more of God!

I stayed with the church, remembering that initial experience and knowing that the Hand of God was indeed upon me in that small church. I learned there what it was like to have clean fun. I didn't have to drink or have sex. I t made me happy!

The church practiced strict holiness. Women were forbidden to wear pants, makeup, and jewelry. Women were also prohibited from wearing dresses that were not at least two inches below the knee and blouses that exposed too much of the nape and elbow areas. Our heads had to be covered with either hats or prayer cloths. We could not be out of our houses after 10 p.m. Proms, other dances, ball games, movies, and the like, were strictly prohibited. I questioned all of this, but put it aside to know Christ. I desperately needed Him in my life!

So after I joined the church I threw away my entire wardrobe that was against their beliefs. That left me with only one dress. I could not afford a new wardrobe; so I relied on other people's generosities until I could afford to shop for myself. That time did not come for years. I wore dresses that were at least two sizes too big and paper towels on my head for prayer cloths.

I was counseled by the pastor to marry Deacon Gray who had asked me, but I was very reluctant. I knew that I was not deeply in love with him, but I was lonely and wanted a saved husband. I also desired sexual intimacy, which was almost at the top of the list for him. So I consented.

The wedding took place during pastor's anniversary week when the church would already be decorated. I didn't have any money, and my family did not agree with the marriage. My fiancé talked me out of believing in a fancy wedding. He also was broke and had one grey suit that he wore to church every Sunday.

I consented to the hasty wedding and prepared for it with only $30 to my name. I actually found a blue and white laced gown that had been marked down to $13. I found lace for the veil and sewed it to flowers that I made from tissue. I used a hair pin to fasten the makeshift veil to my hair. I was beautiful! Even those who were opposed to Charles marrying a heathen noted that I was indeed a beautiful bride.

My mom was not happy at all about my sudden marriage to someone they had only met once, but she supported my decision and showed up for the wedding. His mother was more disagreeable about it, but showed up for him. She is pictured on the right of him in the picture and my mom stand next to me on the left. The picture does not reveal that she was holding my daughter Kim very protectively. We all were sad, but I tried to hide my sorrow from Mama. She knew though. Why was I marrying this man?

  He wasn't in love with me either. On our wedding night he invited another couple out with us, and the wife of that couple was who he really wanted as his own wife. I saw them peering at each other and marveled that these people are supposed to be saved! I didn't say a word though and tried to enjoy a night that I was to not enjoy at all, even in our alone time. It was a wedding night disaster!

I was totally unhappy with this marital arrangement. Charles would always espy other women and talk closely and intimately with them while I would be watching. He didn't care. Even when I would speak to him concerning his behavior, he would just scold me about being jealous and tell me that he would be ministering to them. He always defended his decision to marry me by continuously speaking that he had asked God for a wife with long black hair, a car, and a place to stay. I was his trophy wife.

When we would go shopping, he always walked ahead of me. On one occasion we were with the couple who shared our marriage night with us, and when I tried to hold his hand, he snatched away. He told me that that was against church rules, which I knew was a lie. Couples didn't hold hands in public, nor walk beside each other, he said. He even had the male companion to agree with him. If he only knew that his wife was the reason he was so distant from me, I don't think he would have been so apt to agree with a lie! I had a car, an apartment, and long black hair. That was the description he said God gave him concerning the woman he would marry. Then why was I being treated this way? I wondered if God was indeed even on speaking terms with him!

He would take my car and visit other women. On some occasions Kim and I were in the car with him, and he would instruct us to stay in the car until he returned. He said he needed to get something. He always took the keys with him and would stay in those houses for very long periods of time.

I felt strongly that he wished he had not married this scarred for life woman, but the church we were members of was ardently against divorce. So we continued to tolerate each other. I too began to look at other men, but I could never make the final move to cheat. I had plenty of opportunities to be with other men, but always withdrew before I became too attracted to any, because I knew that it was only a reaction to the hurt and loneliness I was experiencing at home. That's what I prayed so hard to escape when I first joined the church. I learned quickly that unfaithfulness can be seated in seats of authority even in church buildings, but not in the real church.

The first lady of the church kept me in line. She knew that I was being tempted, and made sure that I knew that she knew! Most of the members expected me to go after the men there, because I had a baby out of wedlock, and my sister had left the church in the heat of battle. Yet I was really seeking for more of God, and finally she saw it and embraced me. I am so glad for her! I was really hurting and just needed someone to show me some love! They didn't have to be men; they just had to have that real AGAPE! She had God's love all within her and willingly shared it with me when she saw that some of the very men who were after me were misrepresenting me and saying that I was after them. She held on to me, and I held on to her, until the day that God took her away to be with Him in glory. She was my mother in every sense of the word!

I tried to tell my husband of the advances, especially from those in the pulpit, but he only told me to keep it to myself. "Thy shall not speak evil of the ruler of thy people…" This was his favorite scripture that he misquoted and misunderstood! The next favorite one was, "Obey thy husband!" He had backup, and I was alone (or so I thought); so I withdrew more and more and became very introverted. After I began to talk about the abuse and advances to the head deacon, certain ones became so harsh to me there that I was not allowed to speak or sing in the church. I was blacklisted while still in the pews! The head deacon tried to encourage me and would often tell me to lift my head up to the hills. A female whom he refused to identify called him and told him about my husband's sexual advances towards her, and he noted it and saw what I was enduring.

Charles was finally able to become a little more intimate with me, and I conceived. This pregnancy was marked by great trauma. When I was about six months pregnant, I sat painfully in Sunday night service at the church. It was a special occasion when the pastor was to be ordained as a bishop. Suddenly men broke through the door adjacent to the pulpit, and one of them waved a gun at the congregation, demanding that we give his accomplice our purses and wallets.

For the entire time I was holding Kim close to me and praying. The gunman actually came to the second row where we were seated and shot into the ceiling. Before he could do anything to us, the head deacon suddenly dashed as fast as he could to the water room in the back of the church and held the door that we knew would not lock! The accomplice chased him, but could not open the door.

The accomplice then went back to the first man's side, who instructed him to gather the wallets of the pulpit ministers. He was successful in taking the wallet of the guest bishop and proceeded to take our pastor's, but the pastor pushed him away, revealing that he had no gun! The man who really had one then opened fire, striking our pastor in his neck. They both then ran out of the door they came through with only one wallet as their trophy.

We remained seated in tears for a while until the men let us know that the police and ambulance had arrived. Our pastor was rushed to the hospital while we answered as many questions as we could to the police. The pastor survived the shooting, but was a paraplegic until the day he passed away.

Wednesday evening following that near-tragic event, I heard a commotion outside the shotgun apartment where we lived. A very heated argument had erupted. I curiously looked through my bedroom window and saw a man who had a gun aimed at another man, and the gun went off striking the other man in the head! He died instantly. Again police and emergency crews were everywhere in that neighborhood. I remained inside in a state of terror. No one was home with me but my baby who slept through the tragedy.

My second child came earlier than expected after those traumatic occurrences. Slightly premature, she was much tinier than any of my children, but the doctors said that she would be okay. For a long time though, they thought that she would be a midget. I named her Shanda Marie. My mother-in-law, who hated to see me coming, tried to separate my husband and Shanda from Kim and me. This made me even angrier!

Yes, I was angry, and felt that I had just cause! I felt that no one was right with God, including me! Who cared about how I felt? Who could I turn to who would not betray my confidence? People who claimed to be friends of mine were taking anything I revealed to them and telling it to as many people as they could! I was betrayed!

Charles wrecked my new car, leaving us with absolutely no transportation. The car was totaled, and the insurance on it had lapsed and was past the 30-day grace period. I thought he had paid the premium and was filled with anger toward him. My hair began to fall out, because I was a nervous wreck! Every reason he married me was leaving. He criticized me openly, especially about my hair and that I was again pregnant. The babies just kept coming!

My mother-in-law prohibited me from parking in front of her home. I would park in the church parking lot across the street from her. She would not speak to me at all when we first married. She would just roll her eyes at me the entire time and call a woman to come over when I was present. I soon learned that the woman was someone she had chosen to be his wife. She didn't want him to be with a woman who already had a child. In her eyes I wasn't good enough for him. I withdrew from it all and was quiet even when other family members visited. I just did not feel that I belonged. Now that I look back on it, I can see that she knew things about her son that I was yet to discover, and was trying to help him the best she could. She was just being a protective mother.

I discovered too late that my husband was not discarding the garbage properly, and the pastor and wife complained to us. The dogs had scattered the garbage all over the place, and my husband refused to pick it up, saying that it was not our garbage. It was our garbage! Yet he stubbornly refused to pick it up, but rather told them that we were moving out. I tearfully picked it up myself, ashamed of his behavior and their lack of knowledge that I would not have done such a thing, for I too was blamed.

The next day I was forced by him to move in with my mother-in-law for what some would call a short time, but I called it a lifetime! Shanda was spoiled by her! She just adored her! Kim and I were so badly treated that depression swept over us both and held us totally captive. I prayed harder that we would endure the stay with her and her other son, and that she would love Kim and me as she did Charles and Shanda. Shanda was exceptionally keen though, and she cleaved to me in a very protective way.

Yet one night while I wrestled with getting my babies to sleep, Mother Gray came running to me from her bedroom that she always kept padlocked, tears running down her face. She shouted, "Maxine! Maxine!" I jumped up and carefully responded, "Ma'am?" Her voice shook as she shared with me a dream she'd just had that I stood on a mountain, and a great number of people stood at the foot of the mountain repeatedly shouting "One Maxine, Lord, one Maxine!" She said she knew from the dream that I was a very special and important person! She never treated me the same way again. She actually smiled at me after that and gave me gifts from her "stash" that she kept locked away in her bedroom!

God had moved on my behalf! She and I eventually became closer, but her mental state was in decline. She was diagnosed as paranoid schizophrenic. She would see people trying to break into her home, people hiding in the attic, people hiding behind furniture; but no one else, including the police who were called almost every other day, saw anything or anyone. She would shoot into the ceiling, and her children feared that she would hurt someone or even herself. Yet she was never institutionalized nor enrolled into a nursing facility. They wanted her to be happy in her own home.

Situations worsened after that! Kim had begun to act very erratically, but would never tell me what was going on with her. She was young, so I took her to the altar at church and had my spiritual mother to pray over her.

One evening the mother who kept Kim during her infancy pulled me to the side and told me it was time to leave my job and go home to my children. She highlighted the fact that some men use their children as their wives. I pondered over her statement and made up my mind that I would indeed obey her voice of wisdom. Yet we needed my income so desperately that I hesitated! Bad move again!

What would I do without any income? If I left the job, how would we make it? We had already lost my apartment, and he had totaled my new car! I was walking about two miles to work each morning, pregnant with my next child! We were living with my mother-in-law, who desperately wanted me out! I had just passed the insurance examination (I was the first black to pass it in that company) and was destined for a raise in salary. Yet my beloved daughter was in trouble! I left a very good-paying job, because my children came first.

I had my third baby and called him Timothy. I knew that he, along with my older girls, was very special. He had beautiful black curly hair, dark skin, and an immediate attraction to music. He cried a lot and was sickly. This bothered Mother Gray, and she complained frequently of the loudness of his screams. The doctors could not tell exactly what was causing his discomfort and ruled it as colic. He would scream all night! I was bothered, not because of the lack of sleep, but because something was bothering my baby, and I felt helpless.

One particular night during the Christmas season I sat with him in the rocking chair in Mother Gray's living room, and I rocked him while he was having one of these episodes. Mother Gray screamed from her room, "Get that baby quiet!" I began to cry and pray to God to help me. Then suddenly a cross that was positioned on one of the government buildings downtown became brighter and shone through the door window. I was amazed at the site and at how my baby immediately ceased from crying and fell asleep. It was over! God had heard my cry, and He healed my baby. I never had to deal with it again!

I prayed hard that we all would be safe. I was becoming fond of Mother Gray wanted her to be delivered. More than that, I wanted my babies to be safe. Therefore, I begged the pastor and his wife to allow us to return to the shotgun apartment. They reluctantly allowed us access, because we were their church members. They also had sympathy for the children and me. For the first time in a long time I felt safer, even though a creek ran in front of the apartments, and it housed many snakes. I chose to deal with the snakes!

Timothy, whom we affectionately called Timmy, began to cry again; and I noticed that his skin was breaking out in rashes. He could not eat nor sleep. I took him to the doctor who referred us to the local hospital. They tagged it as dermatitis, wrote out a prescription for him, and sent us home. That medicine made it far worse! The rash spread all over his face and head, damaging his hair. I took him back to the hospital and was informed that he had an allergic reaction to the medicine that was prescribed for him. They didn't know what to do for him. He was screaming in pain and agony, and the doctors turned away. I took him to prayer with me the next day, laid him on the altar, and cried out to God for help. God showed up! Timmy stopped crying, and the rash that was even in his mouth and throat disappeared. God was teaching me spiritual warfare.

In 1981 I was again pregnant. Returning home from a revival in another town in Mississippi, I ran to answer the phone that didn't usually ring that late at night. It was my sister who informed me that my baby brother Melvin had shot his girlfriend four times as she sat in another man's car in front of a honky-tonk on Highway 27 near Utica, Mississippi, and ran into the woods. Witnesses said they heard two shots, but a careful search in back of the night spot did not discover where my brother could have gone. My daddy took it upon himself to search again. For five days he diligently searched the wooded area until finally he saw in an open field a body that he described as looking like a dead dog and was as black as a phonograph record. It was my brother.

Though Daddy was a man of few words, his countenance revealed a level of pain that I had never seen before on this man of strength who could stand up to a gun aimed in his face and never flinch! Yet I saw a few tears stubbornly run down his face! This hurt him badly! My strong mama, though pain gripped her own heart, consoled Daddy, and they both overcame the terrible pain and heartbreak of losing their baby son. Still their lives would never be the same. They were to lose two more sons in the same decade!

Melvin's death was ruled a suicide; yet we all had our doubts. There was never an autopsy because of the gross decomposition of the body, they said. Two shots were heard. How could he shoot himself in the head twice? Years later after being convicted of another murder, a man also confessed to killing my brother. He, too, now is dead.

After I found out about his death, I immediately went into depression. He was the one I could talk to until he became possessed with that evil spirit. He defended me against my younger, but bigger than I, sister when we would fight! When neither of us had dates, we went to clubs and danced together, pretending to be each other's date! We laughed together, and we teased each other! I would hit him and run, but he could run faster! So before he would catch me, I would stop, drop down on my knees, and beg him to not hit me! He would burst into laughter, tell me how crazy I was, and walk away. We both agreed at the same time to give our lives to Christ, which he reneged in, and we buried him. His funeral was closed-coffin and rushed because of the gross decomposition of his body. One could smell the stench, yet no one said a word.

After his death, for a long time I could his voice pleading with me, "Don't come down here, Maxine! Live for God!" Many thought I was hallucinating, but it was just too real to me! He was warning me! My bitterness was taking me over! I took heed to his pleas and began to seek the Lord even more ardently. That's when the Lord called me to ministry. I told Him, NO! Bad choice!

My husband had begun to show up at my job each biweekly Friday that I would get paid, take the check, and cash it. He would pay some of the bills, give me a portion for grocery, and spend the rest. I never saw his checks. This action alarmed my supervisor greatly, but he actually scolded me for allowing my husband, who would be covered with steel dust from the plant where he worked, sit in clean seats and wait for my check to be issued! He was right, but I would always be told to obey my husband!

I was told about low-income apartments that were available to struggling families. I called them, and soon we were in the projects. Yet it was better than where we were! It was also close to my husband's job. He could walk, if necessary, but he always caught a ride. He was not about to walk! We applied for food stamps, and he had to give up the money he was making on the job in order for us to have a roof over our heads and electricity! I would catch the city bus to and from the grocery store until finally someone located an old car for us. I would drop Charles off at work and keep the car for my own conveniences, very opposite of how it was with my new car that he wrecked.

The apartments were rat and roach infested. There were also snakes in the nearby woods. Yet there was a gymnasium and library adjacent to the apartments, along with several playgrounds. So I felt that for the moment the situation was ideal for my rapidly growing family. I then had three children and another one on the way. I tried birth control, but nothing worked! I just kept having babies! My husband hated it, but refused to do anything for himself; so every time he seemed to touch me, I would have a baby.

A fourth child was on the way. This one was marked from the beginning of my pregnancy. The Lord spoke to me concerning her, identifying her gender to me when I was only three months into the pregnancy. When I was about seven months with her, I contracted a very terrible case of the flu and could not lie in bed. I had to prop myself in an upright position with pillows to be able to sleep at all.

I went into a trance on one of those horrible nights and saw a big hand descend through the ceiling and rested on my abdomen for a moment. The Hand then went into my belly, separated the baby, who was beautiful, took His other hand while holding her, and with His index finger He circled the entire body of my baby. As He encircled her, it became a circle of light. He then placed her back into my stomach and disappeared. I knew He was God! This baby is marked! I named her Jennifer Denise; and we all affectionately call her Nesie.

Charles was at first very faithful in church attendance, and was hard on us about it. We were not allowed to stay home even in times of sickness. There was no excuse for us, but soon his attendance became sporadic. He began to skip bible study nights and prayer times, and even volunteered at times to keep the children to give me time to myself at church.

It was along that time that Kim began to show definite signs of sexual abuse. She was then old enough to tell me what was going on. At first she was adamant about not telling me. Finally I used a bit of wisdom by telling her that she would not be in trouble for it. She then broke down in tears and told me. I was angry, to say the least!

I took a large knife out of the kitchen drawer, put it under my pillow in the bedroom, and awaited his return from work. At this time he was on the night shift. Good for him! For some reason he was late getting home. Good for him again!

I turned on the radio to listen to a Bible Class hosted by the head deacon whom I had relied on so heavily. He had a guest that evening, Elder Melvin Bailey, who was guest revivalist at the church that week. I was so angry that I put my fingers on the knob to turn it off. I did not want to hear anything from God that evening! Yet before I turned it off, Elder Bailey shouted, "Don't turn that radio off! Put that knife away, and tell God you're sorry!" How did he know?! I knew it was God. With tears streaming down my face, I quietly put the knife away, peeked in at my sleeping children, and prayed.

My prayers intensified after that incidence, and so did the devil's advances. I was blaming myself for my daughter's abuse and was pleading with God to get me out of that bad marriage that I was at first denied by the pastor to leave. I also stayed awake every night to listen to the slightest noise that would indicate that the abuse was beginning again. When the pastor began to approach my husband about it, he completely stopped going to church. He became very mean and bitter, and I could barely talk to him.

Baby number five came; I called her Karen Elizabeth. This baby was carried under great stress, great grief, and pain; and when she was born, I saw on her countenance that she had born all that stress. She cried a lot also, but it was different. I had learned from the experience with Tim that prayer does indeed changed situations, so I prayed over her every day until

I saw that her countenance had lightened and no longer bore the marks of stress.

I began to have regular supernatural encounters with the enemy and did not know who I could confide in concerning them. I needed a confidant who knew about demonic attacks and would not term me as crazy. I needed help! I had never dealt with demons and devils before, except from a natural point of view, and now I was seeing horned black creatures that stalked me daily! I had to fight!

The Lord had His hands on me, teaching me how to wield the only kind of sword that would be effective against these horned predators! One wonderful night I awakened to the sound of my own voice shouting, "The sword of the Lord and of Gideon!" My hand was raised in the air as if I was indeed raising a sword. When I came to myself I laughed at myself and how silly I must have seemed! Yet I pondered over the experience greatly, for I knew that the dream was indeed reality. God had given me a sword! He instructed me to turn to the scripture in the Bible that told about the plight of Gideon. I was overwhelmed with amazement! God was identifying me with Gideon!

Each supernatural encounter was followed by natural explosive situations. I learned to pray against the reason they were showing up and to note who or what they were attracted to. They were shocked when they realized that I was no longer afraid of them and had begun to cast them out. They then began to try to kill me. One devil slapped me and muttered something profane. The only words God allowed me to hear were his first words, "You'd better not…" and his last one—he called me "girl!" His tone was one of disgust and pure hatred! I somehow knew that he had just cussed me out! I laughed about it!

There was another time when I thought I was dreaming of a man who was very affectionate towards me (something that the enemy knew that I longed for). He climbed into bed with me, caressed me, and then leaned over to kiss me. His mouth stretched over my entire face! I could smell an awful stench and knew then that this was not a man, nor was I dreaming! He was trying to suffocate me! I could not breathe nor open my mouth! Yet a sound came from my belly that immediately caused the demon to release his grip from my face! My inner man was pleading the blood of Jesus! The demon departed. I sat up, still gasping for breath, and began to give God the praise.

Why were these demons and devils showing up in blatant efforts to kill me? Even more puzzling to me was the fact that they never succeeded! I was alive!

Before and after each satanic attack, the Lord would show up to soothe and encourage me. His presence brought me the much needed peace and confidence to continue even though I was in a dying marriage. Yet I was resisting the commission for which I knew God was preparing me.

The Visions: My Commission

It is not expedient for me doubtless to glory. I will come to visions and revelations of the Lord. 2 Corinthians 12:1.

It had been three years since I first received the commission to preach, but God had never stopped speaking to me about it. I finally shared with my husband His Words to me. My husband immediately stole those Words and used them as Words God spoke to him to justify his actions in beginning his own ministry.

I was silent about it. I didn't care at that time. I did not want to preach! I didn't even trust God at that time! I erroneously felt that He had allowed my baby to be hurt and would not allow me to leave the abuse! So I resolved within myself that maybe my husband was right. I could let him do it. After all, who would believe that I was called to preach and to pastor? So I yielded to my husband's desire to be somebody big in ministry. Bad move again!!!

I prayed faithfully on my face in my bedroom when the children would be all tucked in bed. Suddenly one night while I was in intense prayer, the room lit up very brightly, and I could not move nor turn my head from the floor. A deep loud Voice spoke my name twice, "Maxine, Maxine, feed my sheep! Feed my sheep!" The light then dimmed back to normal. Charles came running down the hallway from watching television, calling my name, "Maxine! You ok?!" I asked him, "Did you hear that?!" He stated that all he heard was something like loud thunder! I told him what had happened to me, and he shrugged his shoulders and went back to the television set in the living room. I prayed some more before finally retiring and slept better than I had in a long time.

For days afterwards I experienced the splendor of God's supernatural, followed by gruesome attacks by the demonic. I vividly remember the many out-of-body experiences I had that gave me knowledge that I was definitely marked for divine purpose. I would soar through the air as eagles soar, and then be taken back into my bedroom where I was praying.

Once I ascended on my bed straight through the ceiling of the apartment, through earth's atmosphere, and into what was defined to me by that Voice as "the mountain of God." There was a place of darkness after earth that frightened me. My eyes were closed, but I could tell that this darkness was greater than any I had ever experienced! I heard music that was so beautiful and soothing! It was the sound of a harp, but the music was foreign to me. I had never in my life heard such a melodic and peaceful sound!

Fear began to grip me, and I tried to open my eyes to see where I was. Immediately I began to descend rapidly! I raised my hands to grab something to hold on to. What I thought was a bed post was actually a very scaly hand! The other scaly hand was used to snatch my hand away from the creature that was responsible for the speedy descent! Back in the bedroom I went! I was so disappointed with myself, because I felt that I would have experienced more if I had not tried to see. "We walk by faith, not by sight." Fear disturbed the experience. God was teaching me, and I was indeed learning!

God did not allow my faults to block His courtship with me though. The very next night, out-of-body, I was taken to a certain oak tree that seemed to have been right outside of the apartment complex, and God would again speak to me Words that were taken from my memory shortly afterwards. When I would encounter Him, I was always positioned with my face to the ground, and was held in that position until the Lord was finished with his divine Truths He was imparting to me. It was not hard at all to discern when God was speaking versus the demonic intrusive tricks. God's Voice always left me with great peace and confidence even when He was correcting me—something He did quite often!

The next few days were filled with more divine visions, and dreams. A large anvil came from outer space, descended into my bedroom and went straight into me. God was given me a hardness that I did not possess. He was preparing me for the battles I would face when He would use me to deliver those who oppose themselves! I would be struck so that people could be refined. The scripture from Ezekiel 3:9 came to mind: *"As an*

adamant harder than flint have I made thy forehead: fear them not, neither be dismayed at their looks, though they be a rebellious house."
I was very timid and extremely hurt! God was not only preparing me; He was also repairing and strengthening me for the days and years ahead! Another Word from Him came to console me when I saw how old and haggard I was beginning to look, "I will renew your youth!" He then took me to the scripture in Isaiah, "They that wait upon the Lord

The final time He came to me person to person was for a farewell. He was about to depart from me "for a season." This time the encounter was not in my bedroom, but rather in the bathroom. I was puzzled at that choice of His, but talked with him nevertheless. He wept as He announced this to me, letting me know that He desperately wanted to remain with me that way, but He had to go. I cried! I begged Him to stay! Yet He departed, or so I thought. It was time for this girl to apply what God had deposited in me during those times of refreshing and admonitions. I had received the Holy Ghost, which is His very presence inside of me. I would see Him again, as He indicated to me, but for now I know I have to utilize the power He instilled within me.

After my season of being with him person to person was over, the devils became much busier! Doors levitated and slammed; pictures and wall art spinned but never fell; the children's jackstone balls were being tossed up and down the hallway of the apartment; my hair was pulled and my feet were tickled when I would pray, but I was not moved! The Lord's Voice was not outward, but He was very much present with me inwardly! He always told me what to do about these meddlers, and it always worked! I was ready!

I began to hear women and children crying and thought that I was going crazy. The more I prayed, the more I heard the outcries. I knew instinctively that these women and children needed help, and I was that help.

I finally yielded in 1984 and confessed the ministry and was also immediately attacked! They did not believe me! The bishop said that he didn't see it, but would allow me to preach my first sermon at the very church where I was being scorned! I consented, but was so nervous the week prior to the Sunday event that my stomach began to hurt terribly. I couldn't eat. The first lady so compassionately comforted me and let me know that I had signs of a nervous stomach.

I also cut my finger the same week. I should have gone to the doctor and received stitches, but I stubbornly wrapped it with a white cloth from a pillow case. It was throbbing even on the day that I was to speak. I held the microphone with my trembling left hand and began to share the Word with the congregation that the Lord had given me, "Fare ye well and Goodbye!" People began to shout, fall on the floor, and dance mightily! I was amazed!!! The Bishop afterwards was pushed in his wheelchair to face me, and he apologized to me, in his own words, FOR EVERYTHING! He confirmed that I was indeed called to the ministry and also let me know that when he was about to leave the fellowship he was associated with, he preached the same message as I! God was telling me something even then!

My husband noticed the shift in attitudes towards me and began to mistreat me even the more. Yet the church that was started began to fill up with people who saw that I indeed had the mantle to pastor. They leaned on me more and more until jealousy began to take him over. Yet the outcries of the women and children no longer kept me awake. I was fulfilling the commissioned assignment given by God.

A few months later I began to feel very sick. I consulted with a doctor who had been recommended by a friend, and he diagnosed my problem as hepatitis C! What in the world was I doing with hepatitis?! He immediately made reservations at a nearby hospital for more tests and possible treatments. When they finished x-raying me, they very disturbingly told me that there was no sign of hepatitis, but there was a baby. They recommended an abortion, because they had subjected the baby to radiation. They said he more than likely would be retarded. I immediately turned the abortion down and trusted God that my baby would be alright.

On my way out of the examining room I overheard the nurse in the waiting area telling my husband who had driven me to the hospital, "Congratulations, Daddy!" He yelled angrily, "What you talking about, lady?!!!" When he saw me he cussed at me and told me he was sick of me getting pregnant. The nurse apologized profusely with a red face and disappeared. I exited the building in tears as he followed me yelling.

At home that night I had another vision of God speaking to me about this baby. He again told me the gender of the baby—a boy. He told me that this one has been chosen for ministry and that he would be "a man of humility." He instructed me to call his name Christopher, which means "carrier of Christ."

The following Sunday during praise service Sister Annie Epps ran over to me excitedly and said she had to share a dream with me. She said God told her in a dream that I was carrying a boy and that he is a chosen vessel! God was actually helping me to overcome my husband's slander and aggressiveness towards me by giving me purpose for the pregnancies. Yet I fought with hatred of myself.

This fifth pregnancy was very difficult, but God held me close to Himself. There was indeed more that was going on inside my body besides the baby. I also had tumors on my womb. The doctors gave me little choice in the matter. They scheduled me for a biopsy that would have required, according to them, termination of the pregnancy. They advised me that I already had babies and probably would have more after this one, but if I chose to have this baby, I could die. I always bonded with my babies while they were still in my womb, and so I fought for the life of this baby, especially after the encounter I had with God and the witness He had sent.

Before the biopsy was performed, I prayed earnestly, and the Lord instructed me to go to the very church that I was avoiding! I had to go back to the place where I thought I was not welcome. God had someone there who would help me with my dilemma. I went on a Sunday night. The biopsy was the following Wednesday.

A preacher I had not seen in a very long time was there. He was the subject of scandals and had been ousted from ministry. He was given space to give remarks, and in spite of the snarls and ogles, he accepted the microphone boldly. He immediately called for a woman in the congregation, then me, to come up. I went, but she did not. I was battling with possible cancer. Hers was definite. When I approached him reluctantly (I really did not want him to lay hands on me!) he told me exactly what was happening within me, called for Mother Velma Johnson to anoint my stomach and pray for me. She took me into the back room, anointed me, then brought me back out and prayed for me in front of the congregation. I felt immediate release! He gave me a potted plant and told me that it signified life—that both my baby and I would live! On the day of the biopsy, the doctors found no tumors! My womb was clean!

The baby came. Yet the doctor had to resuscitate him, because he had swallowed fluid while in my womb. They were worried for a while; then Christopher began to cry. Relief flooded my being as they laid him in my arms; he immediately stopped crying and began to suck his thumb. Not another thumb sucker, I thought laughingly! I remembered how hard we had worked with Nesie to break her finger-sucking habit. She broke the habit when she was good and ready!

Chris was a handsome son, and, just as God had said in the vision, he was quiet and humble. He was a model child, and they declared him to be healthy. The radiation apparently had little or no effect on him. We later on saw why the enemy wanted him dead! Yet he is alive!

In 1987 tragedy struck us again! I was again pregnant. I dreamed that a voice was telling me to "call her name Mara, for your experience shall be bitter." I was in labor during the entire pregnancy, yet could not abort the baby. The doctors could actually measure the contractions, but ruled each time that it had to be false labor. Pain was prevalent every day. I could not hold food on my stomach and had to exist on jello and fluids. I lost a lot of weight and had to receive food intravenously each time I visited University Hospital Clinic.

That April we received the report that my brother Robert, who was only two years older than I, had been in a tragic accident. As he turned a corner in his truck geared with monster tires, a tire blew; he lost control and hit a tree. He was not wearing a seatbelt. His body was thrown out of the truck and went headlong onto the tree. He died within the hour.

My sister-in-law and the twins he loved so dearly still ache for their dad who made everyone laugh, and was a hard worker, a provider, a father. That was difficult for us all! We knew that Melvin was on a collision course, but never expected that Robert would be taken so soon. He was the life of the family! We all became elated when we would see him coming. We knew he would have some funny stories to tell us about his great adventures in fooling people! Then he was gone. I felt myself becoming angry, but I suppressed it, because I really did not know with whom to be angry.

In July of that year I painfully gave birth to my last child. Before he was born, the Lord came to me in a vision and told me that he would be a boy; I was to name him Victor. His life and victories would be prophecy concerning my own life and ministry.

The doctors thought that I would abort Victor, because I was experiencing true labor pains the entire nine months and could not hold food on my stomach. My diet consisted of gelatin, soup, and liquids. I was miserable! Yet the baby was full term. I was in and out of the hospital weekly; they talked of caesarean birthing, but changed their minds. They decided that it would be safer for me to have the baby virginally.

When I was finally told that I did not have to return home, I lay in the prep room for hours before anyone came in to examine me. The nurse on duty apologized and said that they were short-staffed that night. I tried to be patient, but the pains were totally unbearable! I began to scream and pray as blood ran from me and down to the floor. I saw shadows passing over me. The old folks called them death shadows. A man appeared in the room, sat in a chair, and angrily watched me! Who was he? Was I going to die this time after cheating death so many times?

My mama showed up and immediately went to the nurses and fussed—something I rarely saw! My oldest sister had driven her to the hospital to be with me. My husband had disappeared again. So my mama and sister were there for support. Yet my sister could not bear the sight and sounds of it all and ran!

When a doctor finally came in, he first peeped at the mess under the sheet that the nurse had covered me, and then asked me if I would consent to a tubal ligation. I immediately remembered when in a dream God told me to be sure to not get my tubes tied, or I would be bowed over for the rest of my life. I fearfully took heed to the dream when I was asked after each baby was born. So again I gave that negative response, and the doctor angrily walked out and never returned.

The nurse had to take over! The baby was coming! She told me to not push, but I had no control over it! He was coming! She and other staffers whisked me to the operating room, and for the first time discovered that they were not seeing the baby's head at all! It was his bottom! He was breach! And he was tearing me apart! As I screamed to God for mercy, they tried to manually turn his body around so that the birth would not break his neck! Then it was over. They had to rush him to another place in the room to resuscitate him. In a few minutes I heard him cry, and then I cried. Both he and I didn't die!

In 1989 while my mom was at the hospital with my sister who had surgery, I received a call from Daddy. My last brother was dead! He too was in an automobile accident. He hit a bridge. Most say that the impact should not have killed him, but my brother was very depressed. I believe he wanted to die. He received his wish. I could barely look at his lifeless body!

He had just called me about two weeks prior to his demise and asked me if I would pick him up and take him to church with me. It was a long drive, but I was willing. When it was time, he backed out and said he would go another time. Boo was the one who never overcame the guilt of almost killing Mama. We all went on and adjusted, but Boo didn't. Then he was gone.

After having my seventh child, I was never physically the same again. I hurt all the time and excessively bled for over a year. I tried to hold out, but the pain became unbearable. Along with it came chronic migraines. A certain woman told my husband that there was nothing wrong with me; I just didn't want to work! He agreed and made me get out of bed and cook and clean and perform… My older children had mercy on me and did a little cleaning and cooking, but he didn't want their food. He insisted that I cook.

I finally consented to see a gynecologist who immediately scheduled me for emergency surgery. He said that the last birth was indeed breach, and it had torn me apart on the inside. He cussed at the hospital staff that did not sew the serious tears within my body! I was admitted into the hospital the same day. They could not perform the surgery immediately because my stats were too low. So they had to give me medicines to build my body up enough to stand the surgery.

Spirits began to come into the hospital room, disguised as doctors. Yet I immediately knew what they were! They lifted me off the bed and tried to throw me out of the window, but my prayers and the Blood of Jesus prevented them! I spoke with an authority that I had never experienced before, "The Blood of Jesus is against you! Get out and go to the pit!" They immediately disappeared!

Another attempt was made. I was asleep from the drugs that relaxed me when I was suddenly startled awake. I looked in the corner of the room, and a spirit full of polka dots sat in the chair watching me. He couldn't come closer, and soon seemed to look up beyond me as I prayed against him. He suddenly disappeared, and a being that I was afraid to turn around to see was stroking my hair. I soon relaxed and knew that everything was going to be alright.

I was taken down to a room in the basement for pre-op testing. The anesthesiologist, laughing with and teasing the nurses who assisted him, injected iodine into the IV in my arm, turned away confidently, and continued to laugh with the nurses. I felt myself getting bigger. I saw my arms puff out as if I was the Incredible Hulk! I could barely talk them! I struggled to get somebody's attention but to no avail! I felt that I was dying! Finally the anesthesiologist turned around, saw me, and yelled, "Get a doctor!" They worked on me until fluid began to run from every opening on my body. When I became stable again, the nurses asked him if he wanted to try again to inject the fluid into me; he immediately said, "No, we're done." His countenance told off of fear and concern. I didn't die.

The surgery was successfully performed the next day. I later learned that my gynecologist had cussed them all out! They were very careful with me from then on.

The weeks after the surgery were worse than the surgery itself! It was then that infidelity was totally uncovered. Also my mentally ailing mother-in-law was brought to the apartment and abandoned. I was to take care of her while holding a pillow on my stomach! Kim helped as much as she could, and my mother-in-law mistreated her cruelly. Yet this time she mistreated all of the children and accused them of stealing her money from her purse. Her illness was taking over. For the first time I realized that she could not help how she was acting. She was sick.

One afternoon after school she again accused the children of stealing her money. This time she pulled out her .22 handgun and threatened to kill us all with it. I calmly told her to put the gun away, went to the room where she slept, took her purse to her, opened it, and there was her money in clear view. Then I spoke more authoritatively, "Don't you ever point that gun at my children again!" She shamefully said okay.

My husband didn't come home for days after she was brought to live with us. He was with a woman again. When he finally showed up, she called for him to help her, and he turned around and went right back out of the apartment. I really inwardly wished she had pointed that gun at him, but he was her baby. She knew he was seeing someone, but blamed it on the woman instead of him and did not hesitate to tell me what she had seen. I ignored her, because I knew the truth. It was not the women; it was her son.

The gynecologist told me sternly that my biggest problem at that point was my marriage. One of the church members had secretly told him about my husband's infidelities and resentments. He warned me that if I did not get out of that house that I would soon jump out of one of those windows! He pointed to the window in his office that was five stories off the ground. I quietly nodded in approval, but did not take heed to his warnings because of the strict teachings against divorce that I was subject to.

I fought bitterness daily. I hated my marriage and wanted to hate the one I was married to, but my relationship with God kept me from total hatred and bitterness. Yet it was a great struggle until one night as I lay in bed, I had a series of visions that frightened me greatly. From seeing the devil and an army of demons following him to claim possession of the earth, but hindered by people like myself who still hold the testimony of Jesus Christ, to actually being in hell and interviewing different people there as the prince of the bottomless pit looked on, powerless to stop me or keep me there, I had a total of four visions of hell in one week and more visions afterwards. I will tell what I saw in another book.

After seeing the last vision of hell of a woman who was there because of her unforgiving spirit, I'd had enough. I prayed as hard as I could to God to stop me from going back! I knew that if I did not forgive Charles and all who I had held hostage by my bitterness, I would be a permanent guest in hell, and someone else would possibly be interviewing me!

It was very hard to do, but I did indeed tell Charles that I forgave him. He actually noted to me that he had done nothing for which to be forgiven! I became angry and wanted to take back every word, but the visions were still fresh in my mind! I just walked away from him after telling him that I would be praying for him.

Papa's Homegoing

Papa was great in age and becoming weaker, even to the degree that he could barely get around. Aunt Georgia took care of him faithfully, and Mama and other family members would go to her home to assist at times. He stayed with Mama for a brief period of time to give Aunt Georgia a break.

I was not allowed to visit home often, because my husband continuously called them sinners and expressed to me that we should not be around them much. Yet I loved my family and wanted and needed their nearness.

On one instance when we did go to visit Mama and Daddy, Papa was there. He took one look at me and said, "Babe, you're doing the right thing! You are living right! Keep going, Babe! I'm proud of you!" That meant so much to me, and it gave me a supernatural push!

Not long after my final encounter with him, Papa slowly declined. My cousin Beverly Wade, who was there as his departing, said that he knew that he was dying. Before he could no longer speak, he would ask her to read the Bible to him and sing his favorite song, Wade in the Water. He told her that he loved her and commissioned her to take care of her son. He died peacefully. Her son had visions of him afterwards.

How I wished I had been there at the time of his death! His life had been long and gratifying, a tower of strength. He was ready to be with Big Mama again. At the age of 96 he quietly slipped away and went to his new home. Mama was sad, but her sisters and she were so strong! Though they had not even gotten over Big Mama's passing, they held their heads up and moved forward. I yearned for that kind of strength!

I began to have terrible migraines that several times landed me in the emergency room. The pressure was too great for me to bear, and my body was breaking down as a result. The doctors first prescribed medicines for the migraines, but later switched the prescriptions to nerve pills. I refused to take the stronger ones, because they always put me to sleep. I had to watch over my children, so I threw the pills away.

Charles began to experience extreme bouts of rage, especially with the children. Even Shanda began to be mistreated by him. A belt he had obtained from the steel factory where he worked was his rod of correction that he only used on them when he was upset about something that did not even involve them. Whatever upset him away from home was brought home to us, and we paid the price for it!

The belt was aged, and steel had begun to protrude through the rubber like little pins from a pin cushion. If one child did wrong, they all were lined up and whipped them with all his might with the belt. I was totally against this action and told him so when the children were not around. .

My objections did not work. He only went to church members and complained that I was against whippings. I was rebuked by the pastor for it, and I tried afterwards to be quiet. However, he one day swung the belt at one of the children and mistakenly hit me. The pain was brutal! That's when I overcame the rebukes and criticisms and demanded to him that the belt be destroyed! Yes, I said it right in front of the children! They rejoiced! Of course, he objected and ranted and raved that I was in the way of his chastisement of the children, but I didn't care! I was going to get rid of that belt myself! I didn't have to. It disappeared. Much later the children confessed to me with laughter that they had thrown it away! We all laughed!

Yet the madness continued. Kim had stood in the kitchen with one of the kitchen knives to her chest. She had a crazed look on her face, but I was able, thank God, to convince her to put the knife away. She never wanted to go to school and threw fits before getting on the school bus. Tim was angry most of the time and began to rebel, even to the point of being tempted to join the gang that was active in the neighborhood—the Vice Lords. Yet Kim was angry enough to date one of the leaders.

I was never afraid of the Vice Lords, mainly because I knew God and also most of them! They respected my family greatly, even though they couldn't stand Charles, and actually became protectors of the family.

So when the rival gang stormed the neighborhood in their blue and black, the Vice Lords arrayed in red and black would go to war, but would keep them away from us.

One evening we heard a great noise of many voices, looked curiously out the window of our second-story apartment, and saw blue and black running in military fashion right past our windows. It did not last long, they soon disappeared, and after praying we went back to bed.

There was another incidence that caused me to fear, not for myself and family, but for the two Caucasian boys who dared to run through the neighborhood! I don't even know what happened to them! All I know is that when they were spotted, neighborhood boys went into action! Dozens of them ran after the boys. I didn't hear about any deaths on the news, so I assumed that they somehow got away. These neighborhood children were angry and not to be tampered with! Yet I loved them, and they loved me.

God had a divine purpose for my long stay in White Rock. That is where one of our charter families connected to our first church and remains faithful to my ministry until even now—the McIntyre family. We also connected with five-year-old Derrick Traylor, a very gifted young man in whom I saw greatness. He in turn attracted his family to Christ, and now he is Bishop Derrick Traylor.

Victor was one of my greatest challenges. When he was just an infant he began to have fits of rage. When he was older he would even try to jump out of windows or drown himself in a tub of water. He gave the teachers a very hard time at school, and he was in and out of detention. They sought to expel him, but my pleas with them and their knowledge that there was indeed something special about him stalled the inevitable.

Still I was required to solicit counseling for him. He was recommended by them to begin sessions with Catholic Charities. It really did not help, but at least it was on record that we were doing more for him than just praying. Yet I was confident that God was hearing and answering my prayers, and as a result, he was still alive, and I beheld him marching with his class on graduation day, even though he had been expelled months before! He had a boastful faith in God! I love that bulldog tenacity that he has! His sisters and brothers pushed him the best they knew how, in spite of the lack of a pattern to follow. They all are born leaders! Victor will make it in life!

Karen was molested by a boy who had joined our church, and she displayed all the markings of a victim of such. She was extremely hard-headed and at times erratic. When I found out about the molestation, I became even angrier with life itself! Prayer was my life line! Even after all of that, Karen was determined to make it in life! In spite of all the hardships and struggles the children and I endured, we knew we all would make it and never stopped trying.

After Papa's home going, he began to appear to me in dreams and always noted of hidden wisdom. I didn't have a clue as to what he was referring, but I kept it in my heart. My grandfather was trying to bless me! I had to seek for it though. I remembered a passage of scripture:

It is the glory of God to conceal a thing, but the glory of kings is to search out a matter. Proverbs 25:2.

God was giving me pieces to a puzzle one-by-one. The King in me was determined to search and discover. With each dream, he gave me another piece.

Around November 1994 Daddy experienced kidney failure resulting from unknown high blood pressure. He hated hospitals! Yet he found himself having to be a patient on several occasions. One this occasion when he was told that he did not have long to live, I called Elder Willie Clemons and pleaded with him to go and pray for him. He did indeed meet me at the hospital and talked tenderly but strictly with my dad. "God had to lay you on this hospital bed, because he's wanted to talk to you for a long time, but you were too busy to listen." My dad responded very respectfully to everything Elder Clemons said to him, "Yes Suh." That was a turning point in my dad's life. His respect for the man of God touched the heart of God. In my own prayer time He told me that He had added three years Daddy's life.

In November 1997, exactly three years later, Daddy had a massive heart attack and was rushed to the hospital. The doctors told us that he had been suffering from a series of secret heart attacks resulting from the kidney failure and the dialysis treatments. For seven days he lay in ICU connected to a ventilator. I wanted him to live so badly, because he knew that I was a terrible relationship. I wanted him to see me delivered before his departure from us.

For the entire seven-day period I could not eat nor barely sleep. I prayed and prayed that the Lord would spare my father. My husband didn't care! He kept telling me to cook! I needed my dad and begged God to spare his life! I was in so much pain from the cold marriage that I didn't want to lose the one I knew truly loved me.

On the eighth day with eyes open I saw in the spirit a very tall, elegant angel with white, blue and purple garments, dark long hair, and huge wings. He looked at me with a smile, then turned and went into the hospital room where my dad lay dying. He was taller than the room itself, but never stooped. He just went straight through. He had a beautiful box in his hands that disappeared with him after crossing the threshold of the room. I heard a Voice say, "I will pity him as a father pities his children." Somehow I knew that the Lord had taken my daddy with him to glory. Seconds later my big sister Alice called me with the news. Before she could finish her sentence, I calmly told her, "I know. Daddy passed away." She asked me how I knew. I rehearsed to her what I had experienced, and we were both comforted, even though she had already accepted his passing and was confident that he was with the Lord. I was the one who was having that hard time of acceptance until the Lord showed me His love for Daddy and for me.

Though my heart was broken, I was yet able to smile. My sisters made sure that I laughed about something…anything before Mama and we very reluctantly left his lifeless body in the hospital.

The funeral was beautiful. Mama was a soldier as usual. My oldest sister laughingly dared my two other sisters and I to cry as we bravely sang in honor of our Daddy:

I shall wear a crown; I shall wear a crown, when it's all over, when it's all over.
I shall see His face; I shall see His face, when it's all over, when it's all over…
I'm gonna put on my robe; tell the story how I made it over… (Thomas Whitfield)

The year following Daddy's transition, we finally moved out of White Rock. The rent there had escalated to where we knew we could pay for a house rather than continuing to pour into the apartment infested with rats and roaches, the children had also begun to spot snakes outside the apartments. Charles had been told of a government program that would help him buy a house; and to my surprise, he took the mandatory classes, and we were approved. Of course, the cost of the home had to be within the range of the grant. After much searching we finally found a home in north Jackson that we somewhat liked at 737 Lawrence Road.

The house was not really what I wanted, but it was better than where we were before. It had only one bathroom to be shared by eleven people. Yet the bedrooms were moderately large with limited closet space. In one bedroom the window view displayed beautiful floral arrangements that resembled a botanical garden. I loved it, but it was not the master bedroom.

Shortly after the move, I dreamed that I was being attacked violently. Someone had broken into the house and was after me to kill me! I called 911 and awakened out of the dream. The very next day I immediately became very sick with flu-like symptoms, only worse. Robitussin was all I took during that time, along with Tylenol for the fever. The pain and agony only worsened, especially in the back of my neck. I refused to go to the doctor, because I knew we had no money or insurance. I felt that I could treat the flu myself, as I had done countless times before. Bad move!

I had no idea that when Kim sneaked out of the house, she was going to get my mama. When she returned, Mama walked in with her apron still tied around her waist and commanded me, "Get up, Maxine, and let's go to the hospital!" With no verbal response, I staggered off the den sofa. She assisted me to dress as Kim held me up. Kim drove me to Baptist Hospital emergency room, and they, in turn, contacted my attending physician.

Charles never came to the hospital that day. Kim assured me that she would watch over the children for me while I was in the hospital. Our marriage was at that time in a state of death. I had previously found insurance papers that revealed an increase in benefits in case of my death, and he was the sole beneficiary. He wanted me to die!

I actually wished he was dead so many times. I knew I would never commit murder; I wanted God to kill him for me! I couldn't believe that I was trying to use God as my hitman! He never did it! Later on I realized how terribly wrong I was to wish such an awful fate for someone who was obviously mentally challenged and needed healing. I then began to wish I was dead. God didn't do that either!

Mama sat with me in the waiting room for what seemed like an eternity. They had no rooms available. Suddenly darkness swept over me, and I collapsed to the floor. Nurses rushed in after Mama's cry for help. I opened my eyes later to a room filled with people and supplies. They had made the supply room into a temporary examining room and rolled me into it on a stretcher. A black doctor came in, took one look at me, and told me that I had meningitis. I was defiant! "No, I don't!" We lightly argued about it for a brief moment. He said, "Ok, we will see! I know what I'm looking at, and you have meningitis! If you had waited another hour before coming to the hospital, you would be dead!" Again I defied his statements.

He then displayed a very long needle that was to be inserted into my spine to draw fluid. That would be tested to see what I actually had. I remember having to ball up in fetal position and was told to be very still. I screamed from the agony as I felt the needle go up my spine and into my neck.

I again became unconscious. I awakened to the sound of much laughter. I peeped through my weary eyes and saw Mama and Kim, along with church members Patricia Taylor and James Adams. James was the church clown. Yet he met his match in that makeshift examining room! My mama was telling such funny stories that even the doctors and nurses were dropping in to listen with laughter! One Caucasian doctor pulled up a chair and leaned over to hear more! I knew they were having a good time, but I wasn't!

The laughter was interrupted by the attending doctor who came in with test results. I did have meningitis, but not bacterial! He said that I had contracted spinal meningitis and would not die, but I would be crippled for the rest of my life and would be in the hospital for at least two weeks. I would have to spend much time in physical therapy afterwards.

Again I called his diagnosis and prognosis false. I was out of the hospital in three days and never had physical therapy for it. I also was not crippled! I had escaped death again!

My regular doctor was a very small Indian woman who knew her business well! After the bout with meningitis she made sure that she saw me often. Charles decided to make her his physician as well and began to visit the clinic after he had begun to feel very sick. He had acute type 2 diabetes! It was so advanced that it had begun to affect his judgments, temper, vision, and body functions. I then realized why he was so moody and out of sorts at times, and he never changed his diet!

It was after he had visited the clinic a few times that the doctor began to demand to me that I leave that bedroom! "Get out of that bedroom!" she would proclaim to me. She just noted to me that my nerves were getting worse on me because of it. Yet I knew that she was not telling me everything. How did she know that my marriage was causing my nerves to crumble? I never confided in her about anything! Yet she knew. She was the second in a line of people who warned me to leave the bedroom and the house!

I began to heed to their pleas after I heard a message preached by Bishop T. D. Jakes, "Woman, thou art loosed!" A copy of the CD was found and given to me, and I listened to it every day until finally I was detoxed from the dreadful feeling that I would be in sin and would lose God if I left that abusive relationship. It took three more years of agony before I heeded to the call to leave. Finally I heard the Lord call out the name "Exodus" in my sleep.

Attracted to My Pain

In 1999 I knew that it was time for me to leave Victory Pentecostal Church. The Heal the Hurt ministry that began as a conference had begun to birth babies. People were attracting to me instead of my husband; therefore I had become the enemy to some there, and I just did not want to be the cause of confusion. I did not believe in there being two heads on a body, so my time to make a life-changing decision had come.

The deacons were instructed to turn away from me and refuse to assist me in any matter. They complied! I did not know what was causing their hardness until one day I asked one of them to remove a chair from the ladies' room that an animal had apparently made his home. The deacon told me that he would have to ask my husband, because they all were not to do anything for me, not even to move a chair!

The chair was heavy, and a sister who had become angry at the entire situation assisted me in removing it. Afterwards I retreated to the altar as always and prayed the anger off me. The sisters followed my example, and soon God instituted Miracle Monday Evening Prayer at the church. It was at that prayer time when many of us saw angels walking up and down the aisles of the church, and even a girl who fell dead in the church was raised to life again. When Charles saw the move of God among us, he tried to join in a couple of times, but the Spirit of God did not flow when he was present. He soon began again to stay home and watch television.

Charles also began to mock me in the pulpit. He would deliberately command me to teach or preach, then would sit in the chair directly behind me where very few people could see what he was doing. He would proceed to make grunts and noises, clear his throat noisily, or call for one of his deacons to do something for him. I am convinced that he knew that God was commissioning me to a higher calling and was fighting it with all that he had! The only thing that stopped him from bothering me at the church was the attraction he had to women and young girls. He would disappear from the church with one of them, and at the end of service he would reappear and try to preach! He also used his study to "counsel" them. Some of them later told off on him.

I continually heard God's Voice telling me to take my children and leave, especially during my prayer times that were vital to me. Preachers who came to the church to minister also spoke prophetically to me that I would be departing to begin my own ministry. Of course, this did not go well with my husband! I hated when they would prophesy, because I would be maltreated even the more! He tried to turn everyone there against me, and succeeded with many.

I knew that it was time to go. On July 18, my youngest son's birthday, I told the church that I would be leaving to start my own ministry. Charles immediately grabbed the microphone and told the congregation that he didn't see it, that it was not God, but that he would not stop me from leaving. The moment those words were spoken my children led the way out the door forever! I was amazed that many informed me that they were waiting for me to leave! I was their pastor all the time!

We began faithfully the following day with Monday evening prayer at the home of Deacon Willie and Evangelist Sandy McIntyre. Elder Emanuel Godfrey did not leave with us, but showed up at the prayer, letting us know that my crazy husband had verbally attacked him, "Why are you still here? You can get out too!" Sunday July 25 Elder Godfrey and his family opened the door of their home to us to host services there until we could locate a building. We searched adamantly for a building, because most of us were afraid of all those animals they housed! We all laughed about it though, but were glad when in August a building was found at 855 Martin Luther King Drive.

In the beginning of the new ministry, I had a great following. People packed out that tiny structure until after months of service, we deemed it necessary to move to a somewhat larger, but affordable facility, which was located adjacent to the first building and owned by the same landlord. He was glad to accommodate us, and we were to later learn the reasons he was so delighted! The buildings were rat and roach infested, the roof leaked constantly, and the aged structure rotted and shifted. Yet the power and presence of the Lord was very evident!

The people we attracted were mostly inner city and poverty stricken. My family and I had spent years in the projects, so this was not a shock to me. The reason for their continuous coming was the shocker—<u>they were attracted to my pain!</u> I thought that they loved me, as did some, but it was my hurt that many of them consumed like a drug! They identified with it; they were accustomed to pain. It was an excuse for many of them to hate. I knew that my commission was not to nurse their emotions, but rather to lead them to deliverance from the emotions. First though I had to be delivered. It was a lengthy process that many of my followers were not willing at all to wait for. Then there were the few inner circle people who were there to see my vision come to pass.

In the year 2000 Mama and I became closer than ever. I was grateful for the talks we had. God had begun to give her dreams of the problems I was encountering; she talked with me as frequently as possible, and kept me encouraged. I had not in times past told her of the rage, jealousy, and abuse. My husband had begun to have very violent and erratic episodes. He was constantly accusing me of being with other men, and would take it out on the children. They fought back. Several times the police had to be called to dispel the fighting. They only told him to leave the house for at least 24 hours. They did nothing to remedy the situation for good, but rather told me that I should divorce him.

One particular dream Mama had shook her to the degree that she begged me to take my children, leave my husband and move in with her. At first she would not tell me the dream. After I consistently urged her, she reluctantly told me that she dreamed that my husband had gotten a gun to kill me. The very next day after she revealed the dream, my husband's friend came and warned me to get out of that house. "Gray bought a gun!" he said. Mama's dream was accurate!

Yet he had begun to watch my every move to assure that I did not leave him nor allow another man into the house. He was obsessed with it! He many times refused to go to work; and if he did go, he would pay surprise visits to the house. Each time he found nothing, though I had boxes packed in closets, under beds, in the attic, and anywhere there was a hiding place. I was ready to go, and only needed God to tell me when. In prayer He told me that I would have to hear from him, or situations could turn into another tragedy.

Mama's Last Thanksgiving: The Train Wreck

I fondly remember November 24, 2000, that Thanksgiving Day I spent with Mama and the family. We ate together, laughed together, fussed a little together, but the fussing didn't last and seemed very irrelevant. We were together—all of us! For the first time in a long period Mama had her four girls, grandchildren, and great grandchildren under the same roof! She had prayed that this would take place, and God honored her prayers. Yet she was quiet and serene, as if in very deep thought.

My niece came up with the idea to have a talent show. The winner would receive a certificate from the family. I didn't think that I was good enough to be declared the winner, but indeed I won. I felt that Mama should have received that award after she very solemnly and melodically sang, "Come on, come on, come on; don't you want to go…the ship is at the landing; don't you want to go…" I wondered within myself why she chose that particular song, and also began to notice that she had been very quiet the entire night. Her countenance was not sad, but very far-away.

At the end of the evening as we arose to depart from my niece's home, Mama asked me if I was going to her house before departing for home. My older sister Rean unknowingly interrupted and asked me to drive to her new home to see it. I told Mama I would visit her the next time and followed Rean to her home.

I still feel like kicking myself for that! That was the last time I would see my mama, living or dead! Around 9 a.m. the following Monday Alice called both Ann and me and instructed us to drop everything and go home to Crystal Springs. Ann kept asking Alice for the reason for the drive, knowing within herself that something terrible had taken place, but Alice refused to say what it exactly was. She only divulged the fact that it was concerning Mama. Ann kept nagging me to tell her what it was as if I knew. I really did know and finally said it aloud, I believe she's dead. Ann burst aloud in tears. She also knew.

A train had hit Mama's car while she was crossing the track to take my cousin to the welfare office in Hazlehurst. She was avoiding the pothole in the track and never saw the train until it was too late! Her fears had become reality. She died instantly. So did my cousin and her unborn baby.

In three days we were being driven in the black limousine toward the church near the place where I grew up. The church was packed with people. They were all there to honor Mama one last time. I saved my tears for the altar at my own church. My older sister would not allow either of us to cry at the funeral. If we even looked as if we would cry aloud or even silently, she would stomp over to us and tell us to "hush up!"

The service was short, yet sweet; and very soon we witnessed the casket being lowered into the ground. Was Mama in there? We didn't really know! My brother-in-law and nephew indicated to us that the train had destroyed her. They said that there was a deep gash that ran down the front of her face. There was no way she could have survived. We had to take their word for it, as we were not allowed to even see her. It would have been too traumatic for us, they indicated. To me the trauma was in not seeing her body and therefore having no closure. I longed to see her walk up to me and tell me that they made a mistake in identity; she was not in that car! Yet she never came to me but in my dreams. She was really gone.

Our lives were never the same after Mama's tragedy. The deaths of our brothers and father were hard to bear, but this one was the most difficult! We each had to battle with mental anguish. Prayer kept me from losing my mind completely.

Ann talked with me after we both had overcome some of the shock, and she revealed something to me that she thought I already knew—Mama had consulted with a medium to get the curse off the family. Both Ann and I felt that she had sacrificed herself to save the family. I immediately remembered that Mama always feared withches and warlocks. She called them "those things!" One particular male who came through before I was born had flaunted his powers and told Mama that he could make her skirt fall off! She said she screamed at him repeatedly, "Don't you do that, man!" He laughed at her and left.

She also had a dream that she died in an automobile accident. Therefore, she would never drive until late in her years when the dream would come to pass. Her fears had succeeded in removing her from us.

Now God is working on me about the same spirit of fear! I know I must overcome!

Mama was gone, and the curse was not broken. The family was indeed broken instead. We distanced ourselves from one another, and mental anxiety set in. I felt alone and broken.

My marriage was also irrevocably broken. It was dead. Charles withdrew his support from us completely, and I was determined to feed my children. God took care of us and fed us daily. When there was not enough, I fed the children, and I fasted. Charles fed the dog, but not us. Yet when people came with food for us, he was first at the table.

I slept in the larger bedroom with my youngest boys, refusing to take one of their bunk beds, but rather slept on a loveseat that was hollow right in the middle! I padded the hole with quilts and blankets; yet the hole just seemed to swallow the piles, and I would still sink! I refused to make the children uncomfortable, though they begged me to take their beds, so I endured the discomfort without complaining. The bedroom and loveseat were ideally situated for me to be able to hear and see in each area of the house anything that was out of the ordinary. I never slept. Instead I stayed on watch duty all night every night. Charles held on to the master bedroom, but I made sure that he didn't bother the girls whose bedrooms were closer to him than the boys'.

After three years of in-house separation, God spoke! He said to me plainly, "I'm allowing you to leave, but I'm staying." That really touched my heart, and from that statement I learned more about amazing GRACE! God loved Charles unconditionally! He loved me also and did not want the children and me to perish in bitterness and misery.

After His bold declaration to me about Charles, my life began to shift! I saw people and myself in a different light—the light of Grace. Because of the rigid teachings of the Law that I had been exposed to earlier, God took His time to expel all of the poison from within me. It wasn't the sins that my husband committed that caused my life to spiral; it was unforgiveness! That was the poison, along with erroneous teachings that kept others and me trapped in guilt and shame. His sins were not my fault; but my failing health and low self-esteem were indeed my fault!

I moved out of that chaotic state and into more peaceful living. A year later I was divorced. I really had not sought for it before, because I had made up my mind that I would never marry again! Yet he was still ruining our credit rating, and I needed a car that I could not get the credit to obtain. One car dealer informed me that Charles had damaged our credit so badly that "I could not even get a popsicle on credit!" I could do nothing about it except to make the separation legal and permanent.

I had to fight for it. He lied to the judge, convincing her that he loved me and wanted the marriage to work. Truth was that when I left, the church dissipated completely. There was no more Victory Pentecostal Church! Only three people remained faithful to him—men that were just like him! I did not want it to be that way, but I knew all the time that he was not called for it. I managed after almost a year to convince the judge that the marriage was over and that I did not want child support. I just wanted to be free.

The church members were gracious to us during our move and helped to make needed purchases. I already had a somewhat new bedroom set that was purchased for me as a birthday gift. I was also afforded a living room set. The house had a large den; the church members helped to buy cheap items to furnish it. Everything else was old furniture we brought with us. I loved the large combination kitchen/dining room, in spite of the aged cabinetry. Above all, my children were then safe.

Even though I was happy to be out of that marriage, I found that it still scarred my soul. Mama was not there to comfort me. Yet before she left us she embraced my ministry and blessed me. I needed Papa's and her blessings for the journey ahead! I was to face much more than I had ever faced before, including many betrayals, false accusations, monetary lack, abandonments, witchcraft, and sex discrimination!

My children and I had fled from the 24 years of abuse and neglect, and yet the curse chased us relentlessly! I was then facing another phase of warfare training that would not be hampered by the spirit that used a husband's headship to hold us captive and bound. This is where I would learn who really shepherds my soul and the souls of my children. This is indeed where I would learn how to use the Gideon sword that God had placed into my hands.

The moment I decided to do God's bidding, the supernatural fights became even more frequent and elusive. I would have visions of God followed by visions of devils! The devils no longer approached me as they had in the past; for some reason they stayed distant and at bay until I saw them. Then they ran! Authority was arising in my soul!

I looked out my window at the falling, but non-failing sun. The evening sky testified against the day's events of stock market crashes, heated governmental debating, marital and family dissolutions, and most of all, the seeming decline of Christianity. These are the days when one cannot tell who is with him or who has been sent from hell to destroy. These are definitely the days!

As the sun disappeared and the red sky darkened slowly, I whetted my mental sword for the night when every unimaginable evil would come out of hiding. I was alone, but not alone; unseen angels who only manifested themselves to me and a few others were all around giving us confidence to face the inevitable. I knew that I would prevail, even though so many of my comrades had already been taken out of the fight by their own doubts, fears, and anxieties. All I had to do was remain confident, and at the Kingly Voice of the great God who held my sword with me would do the rest. Then the battles would begin. They always seemed to intensify around 3 a.m. I had already learned to pray while still being married to Charles; so I was always ready for the fight.

The demon spirits were always targeting my life, my family, my sanity, or my income, and sometimes simultaneously. Numbers of false apostles and prophets came to the church, stating that "God had sent them to cover me!" Because I was still dealing with pain, I was tempted many times to allow them to help me, but soon found out that I had again made mistakes! These false representatives of Christ always scoped out the more prominent members and even took them to dinner to court them right on out of the church!

My spiritual mother, Senior Pastor Velma Johnson, would visit the ministry ever so often, and would always tell me to never allow someone else to do what God has instructed me to do. She was right! So I began to put my foot down on them, including some that were among us, and the battle intensified. Most of them, when asked to leave, would take a few members with them.

My number of followers had decreased; yet I knew that it was necessary for those who were only attracted to my pain to leave. They did not want healing, but rather my shoulder. They were seeking for me rather than for God! I was not going to allow that to happen, so they left with the false prophets. There were others who were never chosen to remain with me. I knew that they were there with me only for a season to receive an impartation from me, and then to move on as God led them. Some stayed too long and attached to me; then suddenly they were painfully wrenched from me. I still hurt from it.

Those who meant me well and were meant to stay were under heavy attack. While in 3 a.m. prayer I heard a devilish voice say, "Don't let anybody help her!" I knew God was allowing me to hear the devil's strategy! After those words were pronounced, I noticed that all who meant me well were attacked with money loss, sickness, and even mental stress! Some gave up and removed themselves. One of them even said she just couldn't talk it anymore! Still God made sure that I have a faithful few, some even charter members, and I have learned to be grateful!

Just before a convocation to which I was invited took place in October 2009, I reluctantly accepted my charge to be chief intercessor. This ministry was questionable, and I only wanted to withdraw, remembering the pain of many others who had tried to connect with me in order to take over the ministry God had used me to birth. So my prayer was one of desperation, desiring greatly for our region to be delivered from fake intruding apostles and prophets. I prayed at four in the morning, twelve noon, and most of the evening. A few intercessors were able to connect with me irregularly because of work schedules, so I knew that the burden for prayer was basically upon me.

I broke through to another realm the week before the assembly! As I prayed, (and another woman accompanied me in prayer that day), I went into a strange, but wonderful, state of mind; and in prayer I sang in a foreign language. I immediately time-travelled into the past and actually saw a man on a very high rock who was simultaneously chanting the same prayer as I! I was captivated by the sight of him and sound of his voice, and I stopped praying in order to hear him better.

He had dirt all over him from head to foot; his countenance was very aged and Middle Eastern. He had a mid-length, nappy beard that matched the hairs on his head. His arms were stretched towards heaven as he knelt on his knees. His eyes were fastened to the sky, and his prayers were those of affliction and desperation. I could see him, but he either could not see me or he was too engrossed in his prayer to be distracted.

I tried to get his attention and asked him a couple of times, "Who are you?" I yelled louder, "Who are you?" He continued to pray, eyes still fixed on heaven. Then I asked the Holy Spirit, "Who is he?" The Spirit answered, "He is Abraham." Curiosity completely overwhelmed me as I listened to his prayers that were exactly like mine! The Spirit went on to say, "He's praying for Lot." Somehow I knew that this was right after Lot departed for Sodom.

As I was withdrawn from the site and positioned back into my little sanctuary, I marveled that I had actually seen one of the greatest men of the Bible! I had seen Abraham! He was so plain and ordinary, yet he is called "the father of the faithful!"

Still wondering if this was just a figment of my imagination, which deep inside I knew better, the next day I again prayed intensely and began to chant in that same Hebrew manner! The same woman along with one more woman joined with me in prayer. Again I was transported to the mountain. This time Abraham was not praying. He was standing in the doorway of his tent that was not far from the edge of the mound where he prayed. This time he saw ME!!! He ran to me shouting, "My daughter!" The accent was unmistakably Middle Eastern, though he spoke English and not Hebrew when he referred to me as his daughter!

I marveled at the strength in his legs, for he was visibly elderly, but well preserved. His dusty clothing that covered every part of him except his hands, face, salt and pepper beard and portions of his slightly lengthy graying hair, also told on him that he was ancient Mid-Eastern. I was in Ancient Israel!!!

When he made it to me, the smile on his face completely overtook the sorrow in my heart, and I knew at that instant that I had come face to face with a father whom I had never met! He caught me by my right hand and led me to the edge of the mound, held my hand up, and then shouted again, "My daughter!!!" His voice seemed to have such great volume! Suddenly I heard loud cheers, then looked down at the foot of the mound and saw a multitude all cheering and rejoicing over me! I was not even afraid of the high mound, and marveled because I've always had a fear of heights! I just felt completely blessed. Tears ran down my face as I was again transported back to the church building.

I shared my experiences each time with the ladies who accompanied, and they marveled.

The very next day at noon I prayed again; and again I was transported back in time to an ancient land. It was not the same place where I saw Abraham; but it was a similar mound, yet not quite so lofty. A dark-skinned man with grey hair, a short grey beard sat Indian style on the ground chanting a prayer that was very disturbing to me. His only attire was a white diaper-like covering for his loins. As he chanted, he blew puffs of smoke from a reed-like pipe. The smoke became circles as it went into the atmosphere. I inquired from the same person who had talked with me before as to whom this man was. He calmly without hesitation said, "This is Cush. He is cursing Abraham."

I was puzzled! I began to read about Cush and was astonished at my findings! I never knew until then that there is a brand of strong marijuana called CUSH! What was God telling me? I immediately remembered something another apostle who was connected to the ministry that was hosting the convocation had told me concerning marijuana: people can prophesy accurately when they smoke it! Then I knew what I was dealing with and began to pray against prophecy that was coming from a demonic realm! Of course, there is more to this spirit called Cush than I care to go into right now!

I left that ministry alone! God actually commanded me to leave! I'm glad He did! They managed through deception to keep a few members of my congregation. Yet when I look at it, I realize that these who were leaving were not progressing at my church. If they could do better somewhere else, then I should bid them Godspeed. I did. These false prophets also began to lure others away from the ministry, speaking evil of my children and me. They declared me to be crazy. Yet it did not kill the ministry. The skeleton crew who were conditioned to handle the pressure without breaking survived the attacks and moved on with me. God in turn began to uncover those who were mishandling us. I give Him praise!

In November 2011 I was on my way to church to have all-day prayer alone. Suddenly when I had almost arrived a man driving relatively large pickup truck turned in front of me; I slammed on my brakes, but could not avoid hitting the side of the truck. I was lunged forward by the impact, and the air bag released and punched me in the face and chest. I saw stars and smelled something burning. I thought that the car was on fire and stumbled out of the car and swayed down the very busy street until a Caucasian woman who had witnessed the accident ran and caught me. She took me to a curb on the street and ordered me to sit until the ambulance arrived. I turned down the ambulance, but was consistently urged to allow the paramedics to transport me. The hospital stay for a few hours was worse than the accident itself! I was treated very unkindly and just wanted to go home. So I actually told them to release me, that I was better. They were glad to oblige after finding no broken bones.

The car was not on fire. I was just out of my mind for a few minutes. My chest and back hurt terribly for a few hours and then subsided. However, the next day I awoke to pain that I had never in my life experienced! Yet I was alive!

In January of the following year I again felt intense pain all over my back, neck and head. In the middle of the night I heard that old nemesis say, "I've got you now!" This time it frightened me, because I did not know what this devil was up to. The next day my daughter Kim drove me to the same emergency room where I was examined and released after the accident. The doctor who examined me spoke cruel words to me, telling me that I was just having "aging pains!" "Old people experience this!" he said to me! It threw me into deep depression! I wasn't that old! My daughter and I both agreed that he did not want to connect the pains with the automobile accident.

I remained silent as he diagnosed me with several terminal illnesses. He counted them: 1, 2, 3… Then he said, "Ma'am, I've counted about 17 illnesses in your body! How in the world have you been functioning?!" He said that my backbone was deteriorating and that my tailbone was gone.

I never really accepted having all 17 terminal illnesses, but did see that the upper portion of my back had begun to bend. I felt that it was because of the bout with meningitis. I had never gone for physical therapy as ordered by the doctor, because my insurance did not cover it. After spending a period of time with a Christian doctor who is much kinder and sensitive to my physical and mental wounds, I found myself overcoming every single illness that I had been diagnosed with, and my back straightened itself! I am a miracle!

In one of my dire times of struggle with my own insecurities, I remembered a song from when Mama and Daddy were alive, and I was their struggling little cripple:

Someone who cares, someone who shares
All your troubles like no other can do;
He'll come down from the skies
And wipe the tears from your eyes.
You're His child, and He cares for you!

The singer of that song is also departed, yet the Lord saw fit to cause his words after all these years to come alive in my heart and give me renewal of hope.

Papa came to me in a dream later on, and I cannot get the visitation off my mind! The dream began in my kitchen, which really did not look like the one I am in now. It had a window view to the right. My current windows are to the left. He was old and frail, bent over slightly, and very sad! I only gently said to him, Dance with me, Papa. I really didn't think he would, because he was so religious in his day, but when I reached for him with my arms, he received my embrace and hugged me tightly! His embrace was speaking to me! It was as if he needed this love! It was nowhere near seductive, but pure and untainted exchange of love! After a few minutes of dancing with my grandfather, I tried to pull away. I said to him, I know you have to go now. He said to me, No, I am never leaving! He was not really Papa; I felt then that He was the Lord!

He looked toward my window; I too looked to see why his head turned in that direction. To my surprise, all of his old furniture was in my yard! He had someone to pick it up and bring it to me. I wondered about how the neighbors would react to junk-looking furniture in my yard; for I had no place to store it! Then I thought of the fact that I was beholding antiques! How valuable they must be! Even a shiny black wood stove sat in the midst, and my son Vic had already begun to fry chicken on it! He left it, and came toward us; but I told him that he has to stay close to it because it cooks fast! He was so surprised when he ran back to the food to discover that it was already done!

I didn't see my grandfather after that. The dream ended; yet I knew that some kind of way I had just been blessed! God was using Papa to keep me looking forward to the wealth of the wise, and to know that loving God and family would be the key!

The fight for control in my ministry continued and continued and continued! Many times in the middle of the night, and eerily always around the three o'clock hour, I would awaken in tears and sorrow. I knew that those who claimed to be closest to me were secretly plotting to take my seat at Exodus. It was so clever that only those who really pray could see what was actually taking place. I would whisper sweet prayers to God; then a smile would overtake the sorrow. I found myself saying, "I've got to keep going! I must keep moving forward!" Yet it seemed as if I was at a standstill. I was losing members, and then gaining some. The income would drastically drop; then it would suddenly rebound! God was fighting for me.

Every time the enemies of my faith would think that we were totally defeated, out of the shadows we would arise victoriously! Each time we were in a dry season, God would always prepare us for the rain! How could I doubt His power that is definitely at work in my life and ministry? Seeming failure haunt me daily; yet I always witness His love in action. The attacks of infirmities were defeated by Faith in His Name! He assures me that I am never alone and that no one in this big world can take my place!

The Breakthrough

I received the news that my mama's older sister, who was very close to her until her untimely death, had been diagnosed with cancer at the age of 94. We prayed that she would overcome it, and she was strong! Yet her voice seemed to tell us that she was ready to go. We were not ready though!

I remember my sister Ann called me in December 2011 and told me that we must contact Aunt Georgia, because she was close to death. I called her, and to my surprise, she sounded good and strong! Yet she said to me, "Well, Maxine, I guess it's time for me to go…" I changed the subject, not wanting to hear what I knew she was saying. I told her that Ann and I were coming to visit her, and she hesitated. She was polite, but she knew that she would not be there if we came. She wasn't sad about it! Her tone of voice made it seem as if she was just going on a vacation! She was a Powell! The next day she was gone.

Her daughters gave her a regal going-away service. Ann was on program to sing, but she was unable to come home because of her financial state. She made me promise to sing in her stead; I complied, dragging my daughter Nesie up with me. I was then glad to be a part of Aunt Georgia's home going service, in spite of the inner pain we all felt.

A week later I was praying and heard the sound of great laughter. My mama and Aunt Georgia had very distinct laughs that were unmistakably theirs! No one else laughed the way they did, and I heard their voices! I also heard Papa's! They were all together! There were many more voices that I did not recognize! I knew that it wasn't coming from hell where there is weeping and gnashing of teeth, so it must be coming from heaven!

They laugh in heaven? I pondered over what I had heard for a long time until a great woman of God said on her broadcast that she too had heard laughter in heaven! I was relieved to know that I was not losing my mind! While we are down here crying, they are up there laughing! I was greatly encouraged to know that my mama, my aunt, and my papa, along with other members of my family, are having a great time! The knowledge of that fact lifted my spirit greatly.

I've had one greater season of sorrow and pain that God has lovingly seen me through. In 2014 the love between my spiritual mother, Pastor Velma Johnson, and I blossomed into a mature rose. I felt closer to her than ever, and I could feel the intense love she had for me. Little did I know that my life was about to shift, and she was a part of the shift. She helped me adjust to my daughter's departure from my ministry, and I was totally grateful, because it hurt. Yet I knew I had to let go. Mother Johnson was ill, but I was sure that her faith in God would see her through to being healed.

In June 2014 we hosted our annual conference, and she made a point of attending. She embraced me and said, "Happy birthday, Apostle Gray!" She was weak, but refused to leave on that Saturday night until the service was over. Monday I received the call from her son that she had passed away suddenly. I refused to believe him! I remained in that state of unbelief until the night of the wake at their church. I walked into the church and saw her body in the coffin and fell apart. My mama was indeed gone!

Everyone else seemed to have been okay, except her sister and me. I knew I wasn't helping her sister Ruthie to stay composed, but the pain I felt was too much to bear. I was losing everyone who meant me well! I was on the program for remarks; I did speak, but very tearfully. She looked peaceful in her beautiful coffin, but I did not want her in there! I wanted her to come back!

A few days later I went into a trance in my bedroom, and God in His mercy showed me a vision of Mother Johnson walking up an aisle. She had a glow on her face, and her eyes glistened with excitement! She was beholding something totally wonderful, and whatever it was, it caused her to move as swiftly as she could, even though she was walking with a limp. One of her arms was bent, as if she had suffered a stroke. There were loud claps and cheers for her as she walked. She was being honored! When I came out of the trance, I felt comforted and reassured. Mother Johnson was in Heaven receiving her reward for her faithfulness. I only then felt the need to be more like her.

There was something about 2014! My baby sister Ann her two youngest children had come home to stay after years of living in many places across the country. In October 2014 she beckoned me to go with her to revisit Papa's old house. She wanted to see it again, along with the other houses that we had not seen since we were children. I consented to go; picked her up from the extended stay hotel she lived in for then, and headed with her down the highway toward the place we once called home.

It was a very pleasant and joyful trip that I was delighted that consented to, because it took me away from all of the trouble that seemed to have been coming from every direction. Ann had an uncanny way of making me laugh out loud, and we exchanged funny stories as we rode down the road and into the wooded area.

I was amazed at the many modern, beautiful houses that had been built since I was last in the area. Yet as we approached the house where Mama grew up, we saw that the house was still the same as it was then. It seemed to us like a monument in the woods, a place that people could peer at and gain strength. A house that was nearly 100 years old still stood! All of the sisters and brothers, except one—the baby girl of the family, Aunt Emma Flowers, are all gone; yet the house stands. It's as if time had no victory there! The house seemed to beckon us; yet fear kept us away!

Ann and I were both amazed at the sight of it! Old as it is, it looked beautiful to us! Ann talked me into getting out of the car to take pictures of the house and surroundings. I left the engine running and carefully exited the car. She remained inside and actually locked the doors! I yelled, "Ann, you are locking me out of my own car?" She laughingly responded, "I'm not locking you out; I'm locking everything else out!" We both roared with laughter. I took a few more pictures as she instructed me; then I jumped back into the car, turned around hurriedly, and got out of there!

After leaving that area, we went all over that area and other areas in Crystal Springs and even close to Georgetown. We chatted with a few people she still remembered, but I had forgotten until she reminded me. Soon she told me that it was almost 3 o'clock, and she needed to get back to her children who were getting out of school. I left her with a smile that I will always remember and cherish, for on November 29, at our niece's wedding reception, Ann left us. She was having the time of her life laughing and teasing until time to catch the bouquet. She raised her arms to catch it, and then collapsed. She was pronounced dead at the local hospital in Hazlehurst. No one wanted to believe it, but it was true. My sister was gone. I was devastated.

After her departure I had a hard long bout with grief. It wasn't just her departure, but rather all the deaths combined. It was just too much! Yet God saw us through it all. Amazingly, after I was delivered from that spirit of grief, my life began to get better. I knew that God was recompensing my family and me for all that we endured and yet remained faithful to Him.

My inner city ministry has been attracting the attention of some leaders in City and State government, who called on me for invocations and clergy meetings. Awards and honors are hanging from my walls and set on tables in my office, but none meant more to me than just knowing that someone valued what I was doing! That someone is God! He always uses someone to honor me as a signature of approval even though after the honors come more warfare.

For the first time in a very long time I have felt loved and appreciated. I no longer feel that I have loved alone; I now know that my life-long investment has spiritual cash value. A huge portion of my life was spent in service to others, and I had no social life at all. There were no dates or courtships; and yet I feel a great sense of reward and accomplishment when I now see the faces of those who, once on the ledges of despair and hopelessness, are enlightened and free. There is another song that Cousin Manuel Johnson used to sing in that old Baptist assembly that goes something like this:

> **"If I can help somebody as I travel along life's way, then my living shall not be in vain." Amen.**

All the fires of hell, the storms of life, and the flood waters of trouble and despair can never be compared to the glory of knowing that somebody who was destined for hell is now heaven bound because God chose to use a little somebody like me.

It took several years for Charles to surface after the divorce, and we have since met and talked a few times. He's still very ill and too stubborn to submit to the help that he really needs. Yet the love of God abides with him, and I respect that deeply. I told him that I forgive him; yet I will never again be married to him. I have moved on, satisfied that the words, "I forgive you" came from my lips for him. This woman has been loosed! I no longer desire vengeance, but rather total deliverance for everyone, even whom people would type as the worst of criminals. I pray for their salvation, not their destruction! Amazingly, this level of forgiveness not only prolongs life, but also slows down the biological clock!

While in intense prayer and supplication during the 3 a.m. hour, I saw the vision of a woman clothed in a shimmering regal, pure white gown—a queen with a tall, diamond studded crown perfectly positioned on her head. That woman was me! I have seen this sighting several times, and each time the vision gets clearer and closer. God is showing me my future with Him! It excites me, to say the least! My prayers are not in vain; and all that I have endured have been for the hour when I will indeed be crowned. Even before then, I will have a life! I do have a life!

This is, by far, not the end for me. In the words of Robert Browning, "The best is yet to be! …Youth shows but half; trust God: see all, nor be afraid!" I am not afraid. I have Sarah's blessing upon me and look more than ten years younger than my actual age! God has indeed "renewed my youth!"

What I once called a time of great darkness in our lives is now called a time of blessing! I thank God for the conversation I had with a former member of my husband's church! All the time we were going through so much, God was raising an army: a FORCE TO BE RECKONED WITH! Victory Pentecostal Church was our "boot camp", and now we are front-line soldiers in the army of the Lord! The above picture shows most of my children and grandchildren, but not all! God has indeed blessed me with an army that overly compensates for the pain! The entire family is comprised of singers, musicians, praise dancers, and preachers; also they are skilled professionals and entrepreneurs. They have sung and played for some of the top Gospel artists in the country, and the best is yet to come! That time is when someone will be playing and singing with them!

When I look back on it, in the midst of all the tears and pain, demons were cast out, the sick were healed, the dead was raised, angels met with us, and God's glory rested with us! We were always taken care of even when there was no sign of food or money! I pray that this will encourage someone! You will always consider a hard time in your life as a curse until you see why it had to take place!

I now host annual **"Sarah's Daughters"** conferences for women along with **Heal the Hurt** family conferences, **Christ in America Youth Rallies**; and my son hosts **Broken Men's Conferences**. I am also called upon at times to minister at conferences sponsored by other churches along with special events. My children are often called upon to participate in concerts, conferences, and other special events in the City, State, and Country. Members of my extended family are grabbing hold, and death is being swallowed up in victory! An end to that vicious cycle of death is quickly coming to an end as they all begin to believe God and forgive one another. There is definitely purpose for all the pain. I do rejoice!

I am now connected with top international leaders who have no need to take over my ministry. They rather are only there to assist me and teach me in a more perfect way to utilize the apostolic/prophetic mantle that God has draped around me and charged me to "be strong and do it!" God has also blessed me with very faithful and loving followers who, as David's men, would sneak into enemy territory just to get me a cool cup of water! They have overcome the entire traumatic backlash the enemy sent to frighten them away from that much needed ministry. I feel the love emanating from these great men and women of God, and for the first time in my life, I feel that I am not just a giver of love; I am also a recipient.

I feel very blessed indeed! God did this for me! He yet has ways of letting me know that He will never leave me nor forsake me. I can feel Him! A woman of God I greatly admire sang to me in 2014 at our conference, "And your latter shall be greater than your past!" Lord, I believe!

There are many more experiences in my life that would take volumes of books to write! So much that I could not say at this time is etched in my memory. In God's own time I will tell more of my incredible, but very true, story! My times are in His hands.

www.ingramcontent.com/pod-product-compliance
Lightning Source LLC
Chambersburg PA
CBHW051542120626
46551CB00013B/1345